BACKLASH
PRESS

A pioneering publishing house dedicated to creating intelligent, vivid books.

Established to inform, educate, entertain and provoke.

Poetry Prose

The Life in the Sky Comes Down Essays, Stories, Essay/Stories

The Life in the Sky Comes Down
Essays, Stories, Essay/Stories

The Life in the Sky Comes Down Essays, Stories, Essay/Stories

A Backlash Press Book
First published 2017
Reprinted 2024

backlashpress.com

Designer: The Scrutineer, Rachael Adams.

Printed and bound by IngramSpark

ISBN: 978-0-9956843-2-4

All rights reserved. No part of this publication may be reproduced, stored in a retrieval system or transmitted in any form or by any means, electronic, mechanical, photocopying, recording or otherwise, without permission of the copyright holder.

Copyright © Bruce D Bromley
The moral rights of the author have been asserted.

Bruce Bromley

The Life in the Sky Comes Down Essays, Stories, Essay/Stories

Backlash Poetry

American Dangerous: Renée Olander
Bombing the Thinker: Darren C. Demaree
Burial Machine: Jacob Griffin Hall
Clay Unbreakables: Natalia I Andrievskikh
Into The The: Robin Reagler
Phantom Laundry: Michael Tyrell
Tattered Scrolls and Postulates: Joseph V Milford
The Arsonist's Letters: Michael Tyrell
The Life in the Sky Comes Down: Bruce Bromley
Unfinished Murder Ballads: Darren C. Demaree

Backlash Journals

#1
#2
#3: Provoke
#4
Isolation
#5

For Neil Merrick and Leslie Bromley Kaplan

Their singing hearts

Drawings courtesy of Robert Littleford

Contents

That Day	17
Gnossienne for Lisa de Kooning	27
When Small Things Loom	33
Getting in, Getting Out	39
Almost	43
Figuring Images (1)	47
I'm Dancing with Keith Haring	57
The Fire Says	63
Wanting	69
Figuring Images (2)	73
The Measuring Hour	87
Albino Boy	93
Bett Spools It Back	99
Figuring Images (3)	105
Beatrice amid the Rectangles	117
Loading	123
Figuring Images (4): Talking to the Dead	129
Figuring Images (5): Listening to the Dead	143
What Betsy Was	159
Shake the Palsied Heart	167
Acknowledgements	173
Works Consulted	175

The Life in the Sky Comes Down Essays, Stories, Essay/Stories

The Life in the Sky Comes Down
Essays, Stories, Essay/Stories
Bruce Bromley

The Life in the Sky Comes Down Essays, Stories, Essay/Stories

"One can only believe entirely, perhaps, in what one cannot see."
Virginia Woolf (1928)

Peut-être les vices, les depravations et les crimes sont-ils presque toujours ou même toujours dans leur essence des tentatives pour manger la beauté, manger ce qu'il faut seulement regarder.
[Perhaps vices, depravities and crimes are almost always or even always in their essence attempts to eat beauty, to eat what it is necessary only to look at.]
Simone Weil (1942: My translation)

"What is a soul?"
He looked up, smiled, studied her face. [. . .]
"I would say—it is what you can't get rid of."
Marilynne Robinson (2008)

She pictured the sunny room, the sun-washed wall, the bayberry outside. It baffled her,
the world. She did not want to leave it yet.
Elizabeth Strout (2008)

Unless you can get beyond yourself, you were never there.
Clive James (2012)

The Life in the Sky Comes Down Essays, Stories, Essay/Stories

One

I'm just an animal, looking for a home.
David Byrne/Talking Heads (1983)

I am includes all that has made me so.
John Berger (2013)

The Life in the Sky Comes Down Essays, Stories, Essay/Stories

That Day

I taught two classes that day, beginning at 9:30.

Crossing Waverly Place, coffee warming the cardboard cup in my right hand, sensing the ground rumble, the sky groan, I saw the first plane hit while turning on to Mercer Street, the second push out its thick coil of smoke and toxins and ash amid the kinds of sounds that words can't quite name. Even though New York University's classes had been cancelled, I went to my first room, where students waited, mute. We were in our second week of working together towards the crafting of exploratory essays, yet the work had brought them back. Before offering my students a single word, I seemed to return to the sidewalk of a few minutes ago, where men and women thronged watching that dark in the morning sky plump, fatten, and tumble to the pavement a cluster of blocks away. Some yanked cell phones from their jacket pockets, scrolled down to a longed for connection, and all swelled their voices at the human sound that failed to answer them. I was listening to the clink/crash of cell phones hurled at concrete as I looked at student faces arrayed in a half arc around me. I said: we can leave this classroom; we can talk about what appears to be unfurling outside; we can go through the lesson I've got with me. They chose the lesson. We concentrated on what it asked of us.[1]

Our text for the week was David Grene's translation of *Antigone*, spare, focused, like the Greek, on what I liked to call the bones of the sentences,

---

[1] Many have commented on the character of the sky that day, but few, to my knowledge, have spoken about the quality of the *sound*: the air that morning seemed so ripe for being filled that it held on to anything it got, any vibration, which spread throughout the body, via the ear.

on their unornamented shapes as if lit by the reading of them. We were moving close to discussing a woman in her world, a young girl in ours, faced with the struggle to hold on to what was fading speedily from her efforts to grip it, that dead brother's body deemed beyond access to the sacred rites easing passage to the realm below, so that the still living were judged capable, now, of ascertaining who merited burial and who missed that meriting, the once universal duty telescoped to mean the right to claim which body had earned the scented oils, the covering over with handfuls of earth. Such telescoping marked, ironically, a widening of the human territory, given the shift from obligation to the dead to manifesting a resounding judgment of the fallen, the godly usurped by the human entitlement to appraise. I wanted to approach what judging demands of us, how it reveals us, by edging near to the play through proceeding, first, to Henry Purcell's *Dido and Aeneas*, to its 1680s sound-picture of a woman who turned away from everything she needed to say yes to, once the man on the other side of that "yes" proved himself so slight, so paltry, so open to a world without her in it, beside him. Before playing Dido's lamenting ode, I advised students to note, while listening, any words carrying a freighted charge, to write about the connections between that weight and the music transporting it, the voice announcing it, to attend to the reciprocities of word and elongated sound that allow players to vibrate across the gulf separating them from mindful ears.

About to cue the last few moments of Dido on the stage, I urged students to close their eyes.

Try to imagine, I went on, that you are a woman who has founded a country, who has carved out the turf of your people and who, mourning your lost husband, finds herself ensphered by the spell of a man resembling all that you thought you no longer wanted, a stretch of golden skin, a resonant voice, the companionship that had seemed so gone from you, its distance beyond measure. Try to feel, in your muscles, in the bones beneath them, the sense that you can extend your hand and pull these possibilities close, their heat sparking your own. And try to recognize what it will cost you to see that his devotion to an elsewhere he has yet to discover overcomes every vow that this man offered you in your mutual kindling. That recognition will be the final series of sounds you make. Listen:

When I am laid in earth
May my wrongs create
No trouble in thy breast;
Remember me, but ah! forget my fate.

There was much, of course, that I refrained from telling them while their eyes were covered by their lids, while the sirens outside started to whine and swirl, just as my students began to write in response to the vocalizing music of Purcell and his wordsmith, Nahum Tate.

In favor of intervening as little as I could in their experiencing the opening bars' slow, downward slide, of taking them to the verge of partnering another body, however fictive, I didn't tell students that Vergil, in his tale, has Dido "falling on her sword," her "blood" spewed in "foam down the blade," as if she belonged already to the Roman world that will, years later, scrub her city and its people from the earth.

I didn't say that Tate gives us a Dido shading into death, her lady-in-waiting at her side, the death itself undramatized by sword or visible wound, as if witnessing the then-current Glorious Revolution and its rearrangement of regime, off-stage.

I didn't tell them that Vergil, Purcell, and Tate show us futures enfolded in the past, waiting to shimmer out into the light, that shimmering is the labor of a stylus, a seventeenth-century orchestra, a throat opened up by song.

And I didn't say that Antigone, that her almost-sister, Dido, both "suffer" from giving "reverence to what claims reverence." A slain brother stinking in the Theban sun, a man who can't make his loving promise good, each teaches a revering woman that she won't be safeguarded from suffering, that, even so, we need—as they do—to speak or sing to the world in which all reverential suffering occurs.

All this, I didn't say. But somehow my students felt the burden of it. The first group joined me in my second class, all followed the sequence of prompts I've outlined, and in both rooms, the same sounds eddied into air.

They heard Lorraine Hunt Lieberson as a resonating chamber, the pap, the nearby pulpiness, the sap of her voice sliding up to the double injunction that we should "remember" her—but "forget her fate."[2] They understood the wrinkle, the worry, in the meaning there. That a person exceeds the mathematics of the choices added to or subtracted from, unmade, the totality of her life. That the sum implicit in the noun will never aggregate her. That she must be more than an equation powered by a will poised to make contact with those events that are its referents, some liable, some hostile, to its exertions. As if a person, as if all of us, escaped what we choose and what can be said of us, as if something always lingers outside both. Many students gesture towards these ideas in their notebooks, reading the words aloud after Lieberson completes the final repetition of Tate's last line, the sinuous curve of her long-vowelled "Ah!" exacting a freight of air greater than one body might ever hold, even if she sustains it and demands, again, that we "forget," lose sight of, what she could and couldn't control—"remember" her *sound*. Some students write that there ought to be rain, that the stage lights must begin to dim as Lieberson reaches the plain of the flat "a," lengthened at the center of her concluding word. And all think back to Dido's song next week, when ambulatory morgues appear below Union Square, their generators juddering in an acrid wind.

We'll consider how the Greek behind "tragedy" points to a phrase for "goat-song," that the term encircles those who listen to the melodic ache of a young goat's throat, slit, in Antigone's time, by a priestly knife in order to honor Dionysus, his powers arced over the Athenian Festivals in reply to supplication, or to the Lieberson who pulsates, in our own, with what she can shape of a loss that her character won't survive. We remember this pulse while pondering Simone de Beauvoir and her "Moral Idealism and Political Realism," where the essay's close insists that living on the ground "means accepting defilement, failure, horror," that the "lot of being torn apart is the ransom for [any

---

[2] I remember a humid summer night at Lincoln Center, in New York City, listening to Lieberson in the mezzo role of Handel's music for Milton's "L'Allegro" and "Il Penseroso," all reimagined by the shaping labors of Mark Morris and his company. She was on a raised platform, just under the stage, and we never heard her uptake of air, before singing. Her feeling-engrained sound was always there. As if being there were somehow a simple, given thing.

person's] presence in the world, for [her] transcendence and for [her] freedom." A few will observe the economic thought netting Beauvoir's words together, a few counter that one example of "transcendence" and "freedom" is not identical to another, or that experiences of "being torn apart" differ, as young goats and individual humans do, along with the sounds their breath supports. But most will hear, once more, the hum that traveled through our classrooms, called up by Purcell's song.

Towards the end of Lieberson's performance, in staggered entrances, a murmur spreads across the air, one student at a time. These murmurs, their graduated thrum gaining force as they combine, make a chorus of Lieberson's voice, multiplying it. Students tell me, in different ways, that Lieberson and her song are their sound-shield, one translucent enough to enable them to see what requires seeing, as if sound and sight, commingling, produced a third thing, amenable to being carried. That third thing is with us as I take my students to the University Counseling Center, as we walk through its doors, hear a great crunching boom throughout every inch of downtown space, and the Towers thud their fragments to the ground.

A month later, my students' essays echo—often slantingly—with everything I describe here. Among them, the finest, by Aria, begins something like this:

She was sitting outside in the short grass, peeling green apples with a tiny knife. Her body is long, many-boned, and in a blue dress. You can see her collar bone shining, even as the chestnut tree above her sways down. My father sits to the right of her, legs crossed, surrounded by cabbage moths whose whiteness waves over everything. Over the remains of sandwich crusts lying on a red/white gingham cloth. Over my father's hair, the color of carrots left too long in the fridge. Over apple peels, over the tip of my nose as I angle it her way. I am almost five years old and not yet so tall as my mother's calf. She has put me in a velvet smock too heavy for the day's heat. But, as I look at her, my mother seems cold, unwarmed by the sun that makes triangles glint on what I can see of her skin. I will know, years later, about the cancer working there, below where I could not look. Now, in this long ago moment, I want her to move her lips. I want her to push out the words that this photograph can't give me, so I can hear them in a world that kicked her out of it.

I notice, over the range of these pages, that my students and I have labored at what listening can give rise to, on a planet where the year's resplendent word is "selfie," pointing to numberless images that affirm their takers are here, in environments that may change, though the selves yearning for the pictures, producing them with a muted click, don't: throughout a multiplicity of places, the self at the center is as if stuck in its singleness and wears the sticking as a kind of badge.

That badge is one of the perils of sightedness for an image-taker who desires that her centrality in every picture should be repeatable, unchanging, even as the locales around her alter. Unalterable, she is what pieces all locales together, or—to vary the metaphor—her representation must be the pivot on which life beyond the frame revolves. That claim equals much of what our culture tells her, in its advertisements, in many of its schools, in how it sells what it busies itself with overproducing. I read, I listen to, Hans Jonas discussing the work of eyes and ears in 1966, an era nearly prehistorical for my students, though his words prophesy the character of the place we fabricate and continue to affect.

"I have nothing to do but look," Jonas says: "once there is light, the object has only to be there to be visible," apprehended "in its self-containment from out of my own self-containment," present "to me without drawing me into its presence." Light and its "properties . . . permit the whole dynamic genesis to disappear in the perceptual result," so that the seer "remains entirely free from causal involvement in the things to be perceived." Vision may secure "that standing back from the aggressiveness of the world which frees" a space "for observation and opens a horizon for elective attention," but "it does so at the price of offering a becalmed abstract of reality denuded of its raw power." We're vulnerable, under the action of sight, to the license of mistaking the seen for what we make of it, manufacture by means of it. Yet that liberty is precisely what hearing disallows.

"The rustling of an animal in the leaves, the footsteps of men, the noise of a passing car, betray the presence of those things by something they do," the "immediate object of hearing" becoming "the sounds themselves . . . the actions producing those sounds," and "only in the third place does the experience of hearing reveal the agent as an entity whose existence is independent of the noise it makes." "I can therefore not choose to hear something, but have to wait till something happens to a part of my environment to make it sound," and "this sound will strike me whether I choose or not." "Something is going on in my surroundings, so hearing informs me, and I have to respond to that change, which affects me as an interested party not free to contemplate: I have to strain myself" in the direction of "what may come next from that quarter, to which I am now bound in a dynamical situation." These are the dynamics so often flattened out by selves unwilling, or unable, to critique their pictures of a world that resists becalming, denuding.

I think of the Simone Weil who writes, in 1942, of *metaxu*, a term she borrows from Plato's *Symposium*, adapting it to refer to "the wall" that adjoins two rooms, to the spaces interceding between one thing and another, that allow all going forth between them to occur and that are "also their means of communication." The legendary Antigone and Dido lived in these spaces, in "communication" with the writers who imagined them. My students live there, some starting medical school, Aria now a teacher who returns to the Indiana of her home, shorn of her mother.

I think of John Berger's recent book of essays, *Understanding a Photograph*, where he underscores that "what happens in the face of the tragic is that people have to accept it and cry out against it," crying out, "very frequently, to the sky," the "only thing that can be appealed to in certain circumstances." But "who listens to them in the sky? Perhaps God. Perhaps the dead. Perhaps even history."

We live in the leeway between earth and sky. We need to speak to it, sing to it, the ground beneath our feet always changing homes.

And, sometimes, sound will come back to us, modified, transformed, carried by the energies in every intervening space.

The Life in the Sky Comes Down Essays, Stories, Essay/Stories

Two

> We have had a place in the universe since it occurred to the first of our species to ask what that place might be.
> *Marilynne Robinson (2010)*

The Life in the Sky Comes Down Essays, Stories, Essay/Stories

Gnossienne for Lisa de Kooning

Over the last few nights, half-longing for sleep, I've seen Lisa as she was at 14, the two of us almost side by side, about to take the front steps of East Hampton High School for the first time.

She's in a lime green miniskirt that stops acres above her knees, the legs sheeny, like mown grass. Turning my way, Lisa gives me the full punch of her Suzanne Valadon T-shirt, the one that shot her out of private school only to land her close to entering a prefab brick rectangle stretched across a potato field, as if we were buds, meant for the sprouting. I find, before her thumbnail history of Valadon and Erik Satie and the baby boy without a father, who became a painter haunted by the compulsion that the Paris he knew should be transferred to canvas, so that his city could never be toppled by time, by neglect, by forgetting, what Lisa calls *my plump gal*: the whole of Valadon waves from one nipple to another, the camisole starting to slump, her ankles bulb-fat from amorous labor, here and elsewhere. A half-smoked cigarette sticks out between her lips, as if she were in the middle of talking. Telling me how she admires the Valadon who loved Satie but who left him *because she would not be broken*, Lisa says, *I like your orange clogs*, her gaze slowed over the socks above them, a pale Dutch blue, the color of her father's eyes. I don't insist on my knowing what the breaking means, and she doesn't ask me. Lisa adds, just as we push through the main door, *look at us: it's bound to be a no-go*, though we both declare, nearly at the same instant, that this no-go may become a kind of going.

Yes, I knew already of her father, the man who wielded that charged, legendary brush, encrusting women in forests of greens and reds, yet bits of them refused the reining in, the being sent back, always, into their impastoed places, as a single arm, one moist lip, a yellow strand of hair glowed, briefly, out. I knew about the longstanding affair that cameras had with his face, sand-white, flushed by the pop of a sudden flash and settled there, on a glossy page, ready for the expectant swoon. But Lisa and I never spoke of him, even when I saw her for the last time.

She's crouching on the sidewalk's edge, years past leaving high school too early, while I nudge through the John Drew Theatre's stage entrance door after a late rehearsal, on my way home. Her long, slate-blue car waits for her, the driver staring at hailstones that strain through the sky and shy over everything, a privet hedge loosening its petals, the catalpa trees dipping their trumpet-flowers to the ground, to Lisa pelted by the wet, her hair standing up, resisting it, as if abuzz with what its brightness might say, if it had the words. I see her rise, turn to me on her toes, gesture at a sweeping bow, her right arm tracing an arc from low left to high above her head. She pauses in mid-air as I return the gift, and we keep these reciprocated bows with us when we move, separately, into the thinning rain.

Behind all this seeing lies the first image I ever had of her. Lisa, at 9, lives with her mother, far from the beach and the bay and her father's studio, which she can't find a way to. Out in the yard, a blond tail's shiny swish and a whinny counsel her to leap on the back of the horse that her father gave her, and she's learned to ride him. Before leaping, though, she tosses her clothes in a pile under an azalea bush that soaks up the hot May morning. And riding, riding through the sun and wind and those little nubs of fluff that soar and sink in the twinkling light, smelling the horse steam under her, his hair and hers white, together, both of them not listening to car horns blare on the highway, Lisa sits in the sway of his spine, saddle-free as she had been taught to, shoved across the many miles to Bridgehampton, where the cops get her. Once they take her down and throw a blanket over her, Lisa's body still says that the moving hasn't stopped. That's when the reporters come, snapping her in half sun/half shadow, Lisa's mouth forming a wide oval, whose sound any camera must fail to give me, there, on the front page of the local paper. But I heard it, and the hearing of it remains a music I'm unable to answer *no* to.[3]

---

[3] This event, and the courage required to embark on it, trailed Lisa. In the busily hormonal world of high school, it rendered her untouchable, beyond the pull and play of much that aimed merely to hurt. Though this apparent

I take that music with me to Paris, in my twenties. Walking northward, hunting for *Le Chat Noir*, where Satie and Debussy played, low on coinage amid the whores, the pimps, the nightworkers caught between having to, wanting to make use of what seemed available, the flesh that paid, however scantily, for what it got and didn't get, I reach the first bump of the hill below Montmartre, when I see it.

To my right, in a vineyard keen on rain, his coat filmy, a young green as if licked over the white bristles, a horse the color of Lisa's hair stands in a dry trough, nuzzling at the shallows. I'm in front of Satie's apartment building, reading the plaque under his window when the neigh comes, after the arching up of the neck, the prying apart of the teeth, the tongue spit-shimmered as it flings out his sound. It counterpoints everything: the Valadon who paced these rooms, so afraid of breaking; the Satie who stood, broken in the gap of her that he found no way of filling in; the moving men who discovered, once he died (the gossip goes), sheets of music behind the spent piano, as though newly written; the Lisa who will later tumble dead to the floor, stalled on the cusp of middle age in her Caribbean/get-away home, an exit the authorities continue to investigate, even now, struggling to make an end of the stories that she gave way to.

But this great **O** of sound, that Satie and Lisa and a young horse gave me, this almost-song, is the gift I go on keeping.

---

safekeeping from mean-spirited antics had another side. It kept some life away from her.

The Life in the Sky Comes Down Essays, Stories, Essay/Stories

Three

The Life in the Sky Comes Down Essays, Stories, Essay/Stories

When Small Things Loom

Oily Spoon:

"I will not be proportioned," Mimi is insisting, "as though I were a lamb chop punitively over-trimmed," she continues, puncturing her hamburger with a knife, under which the spattered plate squeals in rebuke.

"According to Noel, we are real only when measured against the clock; and, really, it is too alarming, Noel aping a befuddled butcher, with me swinging on the scales." Mimi cadences temporarily, communing with her fork. That object, Mariah observes from across the table, is hoisted into air, as if tethered to a vine.

"A restaurant is not a cinema, dear," Mimi explains, making a cavern of her mouth, "and you should eat." The latter procedure approaches fruition as the beef hurled into Mimi's cavern refrains from reappearing—and the fork returns, thankfully, Mariah imagines, to the plate. "Eating is so exhausting," Mimi says, thumping an elbow against a teaspoon, which gleams, inconsequently, in the wan restaurant light.

Watch the ignorant elbow, Mariah is thinking, about to move.

(Hypothetically, Mimi opens the door to Mariah's apartment. She disputes the alliteration in the mirror on the left, near the library, allowing the solicitude of the hall to hurtle her into the bedroom on her right. She acknowledges a lack of acquaintance with the environment and detects a corpulent bureau, desirous of being plundered. She roots out a red turtle-neck sweater, the mohair lubriciously furred; she perforates it with cranium, arms, torso. Its amplitude, as she foretold, requires alteration. Having purloined a lipstick from the bureau top, Mimi besieges the bed in the event that its lunge at reification will prove too haphazard. She is duplicating her mouth with a red so obtrusive that it must find her an inhospitable encampment for the gift, the gift which devolves upon the floor, by the window, and which may not be resuscitated. Repudiating that Mimi flattened on the window, she elevates one half of her upper lip. She will almost bare her teeth.)

The Troubled Eye:

"I seem to be perpetually reduced, or so Noel informs me, as of all of Nature addresses us in the second-person, so that one day, definitely in the morning and, of course, before the mirror," Mimi elucidates, scraping her fork against her plate, which maintains it may be bowed, "we appear to have been abbreviated; in particularly desolate cases, a substitution occurs, time having replaced us, most congenially, with someone else," she reckons, before delivering in addendum: "I believe I've got it right."

How congealed she is within the window, Mimi ruminates, alighting on Mariah in her chair, as though she might never get out. "Identification is always a hazard," Mariah is replying; "with such a plethora of substitution, one never knows, precisely, whom one is talking to."

Mariah's right hand, assailing the table cloth, discerns it to be real, while, across the table, Mimi plunks down her fork upon the sated plate, simultaneously shifting an elbow, the shadow of which inspires a teaspoon to abscond from the table-edge, loping into air.

How percipient of it, Mariah thinks, not to be used.

(In her imagination, Mariah sees Noel unlocking the door to her apartment. He will decline to review his expatriation from the hall; of a larval nature, that saga is not to be remembered. He ascertains, however, propinquity to a bookcase, before which he enumerates neutrinos pelting him, transfixing his body to playing the role of a human colander, the constituents poking impalpably in, out. This abstract calibration obscures his capacity for noticing the blinkered light in the library window, how an office building across the street, balking at immurement in shadow, eulogizes itself in effigy upon the floor, under the wooden table that seems to caper to the armchair, which does not move. Invading a book, he gleans a Polaroid snapshot of Mimi wearing an up-tilted, angular chin. That chin aims itself at the conjectural moustache on the man to its right, who is glutinously evoked due to an emulsive imperfection. Noel's finger prods the territory that the still gummy eye socket, his eye socket, must inhabit. But the socket will abstain from being there.)

Peculiar Window:

"I am living with a stop watch," Mimi repines, disregarding the aerial spoon.

"This morning, Noel inspected what he terms my 'imitation' in the bathroom mirror, gauging its ascendancy as though I had already been supplanted," she protrudes, supplanted by a croak of the clock erupting from the wall behind her.

Mariah watches Mimi's eyes, cowed briefly by their lids. "The next time you see Noel," Mimi propounds, lifting them, "look at the bulk of the brow bone, how it dwarfs the eyes," she amends, assaulting her table napkin with her hands. The linen iceberg, Mariah reflects, afraid of being melted.

She tapers from her chair.

Conscious of a sudden squall to the left of the table, Mimi rises, spying Mariah hunkered in obeisance upon the floor. "A salvaged spoon," Mariah clarifies, snatching that object from the air before it sticks to the ground.

Mimi decides that this is unremarkable.

"Don't let anyone proportion *you*," she warns, "even as a friend," dismissing the frieze of Mariah and the refulgent spoon in favor of her dentist, whom she will accommodate, very shortly, with her teeth.

(Now, Mariah opens the door to her apartment. She is passing the oracular mirror, the library, the bedroom; swerving to the left, she occupies the living room, where she will continue to wear her coat. She perches on the illegible arm of a chair, numinously erect before a bay window, which reproduces her. The lights in the office building diagonally to the left suffuse with expiration, snuffing out the playground of swings below, across the way. Their reflections bunt at the window, feigning peroration. Her twin is effaced by the black swatch of the window-glass: a disentanglement, Mariah discovers, not moving.)

The Life in the Sky Comes Down Essays, Stories, Essay/Stories

Four

The Life in the Sky Comes Down Essays, Stories, Essay/Stories

Getting in, Getting Out

As you remove your jacket in my off campus studio, I note your conservatory professorship in the Romantic composers; a converted barn in Ipswich; an Iranian wife with ballrooms for eyes whose pupils bob from trying to get out, away from husband and twin daughters and the Ipswich barn, which she can't convert to Tehran: to the heat, the market place, the Caspian Sea. It's hot, you say, looking at my radiators, forgetting the December outside that I don't let in.

Your wife brought you an egg salad sandwich, the single time I saw her. We were at choir practice, You pumped the keys of Harvard's Busch-Reisinger organ—and didn't thank her. She tightened her mouth; she left.

Do you mind, you ask, unbuttoning your shirt, when I think of Freud and my father and the fist I knew of him, while my mother sat up straight at the kitchen table, tightening her mouth, guarding her teeth. I see: a home-movie of a knee high boy in a play pen, groping for that silver ash tray on the nearby table, stealing it, biting it with teeth not quite there. Beyond the Freud who proposes father-substitution—always carnal, always misguided—as the source of what will be about to happen, beyond taking off your shirt, you wear the unavailableability of an Ipswich barn and the wife who wants to leave you, but won't. You met her while expounding Liszt at the American University in Tehran. She lured you with the shimmer of her hair, you remember, adding quickly that you should make the 4 p.m. train. But you close your eyes once I have you in my mouth, and I am in my imperceptible pen, wanting, not wanting, to get out.

The Life in the Sky Comes Down Essays, Stories, Essay/Stories

Five

The Life in the Sky Comes Down Essays, Stories, Essay/Stories

Almost

She thought that she wanted him to stay in the same place, but she didn't know where that place was.

She wanted to be able to return to him, to come back with bags of vegetables, coffee, and cheese, to open their apartment door and smell the rosemary soap he showered with on weekday evenings, before Noah was born. She would track him through the kitchen and down the hall, into the living room where he would be standing before the window, spotting the snow that must be about to fall. The back of his legs would glisten with water that hadn't dried. She touched his tail bone with her hand: "Keep it there," he said, the bone screened by her hand.

She couldn't protect him.

She carries the weekend shopping up the stairs, imagining the scene behind her apartment door. Louisa, her husband's mother, would have wanted to read to Noah, but she chose, as usual, to do her nails. Noah is evaluating a monster movie in which the dead stalk the living in houses whose cardboard walls are about to come down. "Stop jiggling on the bed," Louisa insists, the nail polish shaking to the floor. "They all look alike," Noah replies, referring to the living and the dead. He won't be interested in distinguishing them; he won't hear her key twisting in the lock.

When she opens the door, Noah is at the kitchen table, scratching paper with a crayon. Red and shaped like a missile, the crayon dwarfs his right hand.

"Did it hurt him?" Noah asks, shuddering the table as he draws.

"Where's your grandmother?" she responds, trying not to look down. She pulls at the refrigerator and finds his half-eaten tuna sandwich on a shelf, next to an empty pint of apple juice.

"You drank your juice," she says, facing the back of his neck, exposed by the shortness of his hair. She sees herself wanting to shield it with her hand.

"Look," he directs her, holding up the paper cemetery of stick men without heads, without clothes, piled at the bottom of the page. Their heads seem to bounce in the upper right-hand corner, as though they had been bowled there.

"It hurt," he tells her, giving her the paper and the crayon.

When she looks in her bedroom, her husband's mother is lying on the bed, asleep, painted nails leaning on her thighs. Disturbed by the pillow, Louisa's hair crouches on her face, shadowing the vertical line between her eyebrows, so that the line merges with her nose. Her lips are the color of her nails, smudged at the corners, as though she had been caught in a murmur between one word and another. A woman on the television sprays kitchen stains with an aerosol that encourages the stains to disappear. Turning off the television, she notices how the polish puckers at Louisa's cuticles, emphasizing the grey, ridged skin below them. It will be time to wake her.

But she doesn't wake her.

What she wants, when she enters the living room, is not to remember the ruin of the car, the ruin of his face that she couldn't identify under one of the wheels, as if the car had birthed him on a road from which he wouldn't rise. She wants to forget the duplicates of his face stiffening in picture frames on tables she can't yet discern. She wants to walk through the room and approach the window, while in the apartments overlooking the park, lights blink on, disclosing the snow that doesn't fall, the anonymous father and son parking a car that won't engulf them, permitting them to move up the brownstone's steps that are always there. She wants to wake Louisa and send her home. She wants to sit at a table with Noah and draw a body uniformly whole. It won't smell of rosemary soap or require the kind of protection that was beyond her. Together, they'll position it on the page, and to them it will seem almost incapable of breaking.

Six

The Life in the Sky Comes Down Essays, Stories, Essay/Stories

Figuring Images (1)

Following Simone Weil in *Attente de Dieu*, if we want to declare that "le regard est ce qui sauve," that it's desire "qui sauve," we must identify the labor in looking, we must know what we are saving, and how desire can become the agent of our delivery.

Solely by that work will our form-making, our image-making, serve us. These words postulate that our pictures portend a route to future action, that they chart the hypothesis of an achieved exertion, rendering the future and the past correlative and attesting—in their visuality—to a kinship with the world that compasses them. But Proust's imaging power, in *Contre Sainte-Beuve*, for instance, documents the ache for a pre-lapsarian terrain that readers, in our unending lateness, penetrate by virtue of a divinatory seeing in contradistinction to Weil's counsel: "nous ne pouvons pas faire même un pas vers le ciel." So long as we can't take a single step towards heaven, with ownership of that region as our goal, towards the sky that will abidingly surpass us, so long as "la direction vertical nous est interdite," we ought to share in the ache and correct its picture, recognize the vertical avenue of our pining yet honor our interdiction from fusing with what we can't lay claim to. To mime the unifying force of a realm before the Fall, to ape the coalition anterior to our descent into time, is to aspire to supplant it—to establish the self as the irrigator of all phenomena. That which opposes the summational image, however, won't be exchanged for its representations; a tropism may ease us in the direction of exchange, but "toutes les sources de puissance" lie "hors de ce monde," outside this world, which, nevertheless, is saturated with signs of power-sources that we can't track. Facing that inability to track, we need at once to concede our tropism and to reorient its turning in order to announce "le oui nuptial," the nuptial *yes* that Weil and Virginia Woolf urgently conjure for us. We need to pledge ourselves to conceptualizing the act of picturing in another way.

As a means of clarifying the tasks inherent in such a promise, I ruminate on desire, on power, on the thinking recumbent in them, on their visual representations that so often structure the ways in which we project ourselves into the continuous space we denominate as world. Doing so, I posit the reciprocity of mind and body, the complementary character of mental actions and the physical behaviors incited by them. If, with Woolf—in "Memories of a Working Women's Guild"—I wish to say that "after all, the imagination is largely the child of the flesh," I should apprehend that when I think, my body thinks with me, that what I picture to myself is coincident with the corporeality I consign myself to knowing. How we conceptualize, how we grow round with thought and with thought's behavioral coordinates, all superintend our negotiation of the world, whose spatial continuity our pensive "flesh" can never conclusively encompass. If these statements are true, if with Weil we appoint imagination "la source des actions," to retrain our capacity for imagination would be to re-envisage what it means to act. But, since desire undergirds imaginative operations, enkindles the "flesh" in which they occur, vitalizes the gaze we pitch at the object of our yearning, we ought to examine what desire appears to dictate to us. Precisely to the extent that we can do this may we claim our embarkation on the toil of a revised looking.

Because of desire's appetitive properties, because of its hankering for the ingestion of its object, we often behave as though to absorb were necessarily not to think. In consequence, the thing for which we crave, intagliated with a beauty our longing exerts itself to reach, vanishes from sight once we swallow it. The finality we imitate here, however, indicates an energy whose reapplication would ensue if we were to educate, again, our manner of directing it.

Our treatment of beauty can commend us to that undertaking when, like Weil, we regard beauty as the sole finality here below: while we are drawn towards it "sans savoir quoi lui demander," we may nevertheless replace our facility for interrogation with what we can do to the thing which seems to offer us "sa proper existence." But "la grande douleur de la vie humaine" is that looking and eating "soient deux" different operations, so that perhaps vice, depravity, and crime, "dans leur essence," manifest our straining to eat beauty—to eat what we should only "regarder." Eve, as Weil suggests, may have caused humanity to be lost by eating the fruit, though "l'attitude inverse," looking at the fruit "sans le manger," might be what is required to save it.

Rather than hungering for a Proustian repossession of the lost, we must acquiesce in asking what we intend to point to by the terminological network of desire, power, the cognitive actions in which both originate, and by the objects outside any network. We must distance ourselves, in so far as we can, from our entanglement in *how* we see in order to attain to the personhood indispensable for ample vision. Following these imperatives, to save our personhood is to dispossess ourselves of what we thought we knew of it. And aiming our desire—our re-schooled longing—at dispossession, we liberate objects and world from our engorgement.

Such liberation results from the "no" implicit in "le oui nuptial," the "no" which shuns the compulsion of our fancy to enchain its referents to the pictures we fabricate of them. Repealing enchainment, we prepare ourselves for committal to a "yes" which establishes a rift, of whatever size, between our desires and their satisfaction—between the mental, verbal, pictorial images forged by our cupidity and the target of unceasing space, for which those images will always be inadequate substitutes. But inadequacy of fit, of accordance, both demonstrates a breach and rescues the world from the rule that it should correspond to what we demand of it, so that our sense of inadequacy reveals a gulf in which the world may be said to happen and readies us for what Weil terms "la destruction" of the selves we thought we were. In denying ourselves, in challenging what those selves manufacture, we become capable of founding "un autre" by means of a creative affirmation: "on se donne" in ransom "pour l'autre"; we empty ourselves in an effort to redeem the "otherhood" accessible to us and whose magnitude our eyes uncover, when rightly used. Yet this right-use involves our unchaining what we designate as power and desire from the teleological thinking to which we affix them.

If my love of power amounts to a desire to institute "un ordre" among the people and things around me, my predilection for order springs from what I particularize by the name of beauty. Nevertheless, my unsatisfied appetite, the mandate that the ring of my hunger must go on increasing, heralds my need for contact with what Weil calls the beauty of the universe, which, on the strength of its dimensional scale, eludes the snare of my encircling. Because our manner of disposing such hoped for order is unequal to the world, it can only hide it; and, for us, the propriety of the world's concealment consists in its rallying our skill at untying desire from both dilation and fulfillment. So loosed from the cordon we've made, we face the very attention, animated by desire, that we never thought we stood in need of.

This integration of desire and attention takes me to Paul Engelmann's proposal that, though "true propositions form a picture of the world, they can say nothing about their own relation" to it, "by virtue of which they are its picture." Despite the assurance of that claim, when dispossessed of an acquisitive selfhood, when emptied of the desire that recognizes itself by what it eats, we are free to attend to the world's disengagement from equivalence to our pictures of it. Yet the difference between world and picture doesn't demolish relation but provokes our assembling it, if by "relation" we signify something other than identity's noose. Broken, voided of concepts we could never use under the name of legitimacy, we look out—at the shock produced by a new breed of image. And Woolf reminds us how to condition the venture of our looking.

Before probing a little further the ways in which Woolf prepares us for reviewing the individual and what he sees, I want to acknowledge the criteria that determine the utility of self-emptying, of self-dislodgement, since for Weil and Woolf those criteria seem so distinguishable. Both consider desires which must be thwarted, flouted, reoriented in the face of things, whether Eve's fruit or the "large earthenware pot," whose clay, under the work of human hands, evolves into another kind of fruit and so signals the materiality of generative things in Woolf's "Robinson Crusoe," from *The Second Common Reader*. Both connect desires, the conceptual activities fuelled by them, and the imaging capacities we train on the solidity of the world; both imply that we see, we look, we behave, owing to the charges inherent in this connective network, out of which we fashion essays, stories, novels, paintings that tell of that conduction—each a goad to potential readerly behaviors as each originates in the world wide enough to include it. And both disdain, implicitly, Proust's *eidolopoeia*, his form-making, which, by its picturing will, wishes to return the always vanished to a self already dead because of the circular character of its thinking, because circularity, here, supposes that the world will adhere to the circumference of its injunction. Yet, for Weil and Woolf, the primacy of any image—verbal, pictorial, sonic, all bent upon by mind—is its failing to wind itself round the world of things, so that we judge an image worthy due to its incapacity for, its rejection of, total comprehensiveness. And such incapacity renders Engelmann's "relation" an avowal of the not-to-be-captured: the educative image turns me towards what it can't wholly show, towards the incalculable on the other side of it, conducing to my awareness of the "other world" vital to Woolf's "Walter Sickert," whose capaciousness embraces even its failed representations.

But the ends of conduction, for Weil, for Woolf, appear distinct. If we must refrain from positioning ourselves "au centre de l'espace," which Weil holds in her *American Notebooks*, published as *La Connaissance surnaturelle*, our forbearance reprehends a perspective that seems to install us there, at the hub of the real. Yet the very "condition de la perception," the very requisite for seeing the real, extorts from us our emplacement at the heart of it. To surmount "la perspective" is to recognize no center in the world, only outside "du monde," in order—through love of God— that we should renounce the illusory power he has left to us of saying "je suis." Any picture that fosters such renunciation merits the labor of our gaze and angles us towards what won't be framed by it. I think, now, in regard to Weil's "justice surnaturelle" and to the God who is its origin, of James Hillman's exploration of the mythic in *A Terrible Love of War*, seeing that myth shepherds in the lexicon of the unfathomable, which organizes Weil's experience of theodicy.

Hillman envisions "myths" as the "norms of the unreasonable," whose "effect" plunges us into feeling that there is "no way out," if "out" describes a terrain beyond their purview. Before our lack of egress, before the "necessity" which overhangs us, we must take a "leap of imagination" into "myth," into the "meaning without explanation" on which, for example, Bernard and Woolf herself predicate the "'methodical absorption'" so fundamental to the images in *The Waves*. Though Woolf doesn't syllable Weil's God, she nevertheless advances characters who address "'what is abstract'" at the "'end of the avenue, in the sky,'" who struggle to "'find something unvisual beneath'" the solidity they see—an effort as "unreasonable," as beyond reason, as Weil's argued for perspectival shift. Like the Bernard who walks through the National Gallery "'picking up fragments'" while he craves for wholes, like Defoe as he presents us with a "large earthenware pot" whose reality is attributable to the background which must outreach it, we stand steeped in a world braced by the "'unvisual,'" by what we can never claim to see absolutely, beyond sounding. Even so, our paintings (our images) intimate what they can't measure if their makers and viewers abide in the "'perpetual solicitation of the eye,'" "'methodical'" when it adds "'stroke to stroke,'" look to look, outside the incantation of a mere "I am." Both Weil and Woolf would assert that, so abiding, we edge near to the justice of which we are capable.

And they would be right.

The Life in the Sky Comes Down Essays, Stories, Essay/Stories

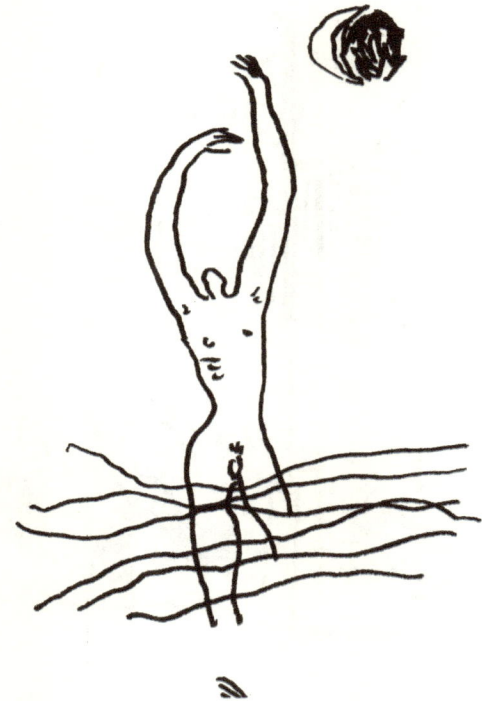

Seven

The world we are born into is not the one we leave.
Mary Ruefle (2012)

The Life in the Sky Comes Down Essays, Stories, Essay/Stories

I'm Dancing with Keith Haring

1938's *Marie Antoinette* burbles up another ball scene on the television aspark in a corner of the bedroom, to the right of the wall of windows looking out, if windows, like eyes, can look out, on the red-bricked junior high school shut because of too many lousy student/teacher performances. Neil sees that I'm busy with what he calls my *vertical dreaming* again, standing, looking but discovering something else, certainly not the dauphine of France about to meet Count Fersen, or Tyrone Power in thigh-tight leggings, ready to gamble on a Swedish accent that fails to show.

    Standing, I dream of my body without clothes lying face up in bed, cock mustering to attention, that bedded Bruce somehow fissioned from the one who lingers, hypnotized before the windowed wall, his back to its rectangular panes that shiver from a gusty whirl of air seeming to twitch the street lights on, while both Bruces persist in a doubled sort of *there*. We're twinned and weightless, he and I, that lack of weight announcing the failure to find another way: to be one thing without the semi-solace of forgiveness for some misremembered flaw or a fulfillment whose demands, the two Bruces think, would only not support its continuing to last. The cipher on the bed begins to blur away when Neil moves a hand up to my right shoulder, night nosing at the windows behind us, as if it wanted to come in. And the too young dauphine, played by a slim though middle-aged Norma Shearer, squints at Fersen through her mask, her teeth silvery with spit and dessert wine.

    Tyrone Power, once allowed, will drink it all.

    Before this can happen, the orchestra squelches out a dance that means to mime Rameau but becomes a Gershwinesque mush of bottom heavy strings topped by piccolo fanfares. The sound stretches between two discrete time-scales, a discord Neil notes as I check my outfit in the full-length mirror before we call the cab that will take us to a 1980s retro night at The Fire House, once The Vestry, once a church whose soup kitchen lines roped around all four blocks, giving God's house a hungry pull.

Upright, dreaming, I gaze at the crowded glass. My almost 50 year old body stands alongside the near adult I then was, spotting Neil on desanctified ground under a disco's strobe light flash, unzipped flies inviting the hoist and hump of pelvis-on-pelvis, as Grace Jones demanded, in song, that we should *pull up to the bumper, baby*, all the world an outside through which everyone ought to be capable of moving. Years afterwards, Neil window-dresses Barneys New York street-level displays, and I sink myself into teaching approaches to critical thought at the university downtown. Yet the mirror affirms that the two Bruces, together, can still slide on these Gaultier striped tights, this Westwood silk jacket, these steel-capped, platform ankle boots. Turning to the screen before Neil flicks it off, I speculate that Norma Shearer must be unable to move in her square-tipped shoes, shrinking under the carapace of her gown, seamed with celluloid diamonds up to the cleavage, fossilized by powder. Antoinette could register Versailles lacquered on pasteboard windows if she turned, but the polyp-like wig sequesters her from turning. If she were to implode, the wig would stand. Even so, Tyrone and Norma bend towards each other; the gavotte begins; in the taxi with Neil, I think of cinematic dances unending on other screens—and of Carl, who became Keisho because he hated the memories buried in his name.

The Keisho I thought I knew made an idol of Rei Kawakubo. He worshipped it daily in his job pushing menswear at Comme des Garçons, threading stories about the magazine-friendly faces that came to him, about Julian Sands slumped in a dressing room, bewitched by his own sockless feet for time without measure; about the titled British lady who, in another age, had been stuck to Mick Jagger's side but who now crackled out Lou Reed songs, while her band scratched at their guitars. She would tilt towards the wall-high mirror, in a man's suit slit diagonally from nipple to mid-thigh, murmuring endearments to herself as though that image gave her back someone other, someone worthy of being fused to. Keisho spun these tales in the store's stockroom, at a marbled white table before a window so wide that it was a flatscreen on which the Kawakubo-designed courtyard rose up: three dwarfed trees, a curve of water around them, its petalled surface flaring red from lights in the mud below. But this hip-swirling star of The Vestry's early morning hours, this talking Keisho, was back-storied by Carl Thomas from the Bronx. Surging up under a mother's insistence that he would forever be insufficiently black and beautiful, Carl was overmastered by his father's affection for sucking what he called *the love juice* out of him, the father who schooled two older sons in committing identical lessons, even as all three, I soon learned, berated Carl for being bleached from the womb a pale nut brown. So, he lopped off Carl and Thomas and grew into Keisho from Brazil, raised in the shadow of the mound that hulks over São Paulo, its shops shimmered by a sun that won't go down. Ahead, however, of his Vestry stardom, long before Neil and I are gliding through the swung open doors of The Fire House, Keisho/Carl will die of pancreatitis in an uptown hospital. The doctors reported, after opening him up: *there was so little to him that he seemed already gone*, though I remember Keisho's yearning for the far, for the distant, for any world away from the Carl who had been extinguished.

In the club now, parallel to Bryan Ferry's croon, I hear Keisho chanting out his manhunt call of *you got the goo I need*. But that's when Keith Haring appears to ascend from the floor, as if alive.

He's been crotch-thumping the stone beneath our feet in satin shorts that stop at the knee, his calf muscles long and quivering to the bass line tune of blood in my ears, torso bare, the tits poking up, his arms fibred with brownish veins in the shape of tobacco leaves. He'd surely taste of honeysuckle if you were to lick him, unmarked by the disease that bedeviled those *needle lovers* and *buttboys* belonging to what my students go on to identify as *the old times*, pertly reordering a world they can't concentrate on enough to recognize, due to its inadmissibility.[4] Swaying below the mirror ball that used to summon Keisho's power to picture a Carnival in Rio he'd never quite seen, I don't know what this Keith Haring is—under the lemon-lightened quiff, under the awning of his name that keeps curlicues of painted dicks and breasts entwining on more

---

[4] My students at New York University still have a tough time with AIDS and its histories. Much of their writing about work by Randy Shilts, Richard Rodriguez, and David Wojnarowicz proceeds as if the past no longer lived here, in varied form, in the present. But it does, and a few of them yield to that awakening.

museum walls than anyone can hope to count. What I know is that life's little word aims at something larger than I'll ever learn to carry. I know that Neil and I are dancing, balls to balls, in time with Chaka Khan's ecstatic wail, when Keith Haring uplifts his leafy arms as if everything were here, an early sun just flickering at the repurposed windows of the church, even if no one in The Fire House has yet begun to see it.

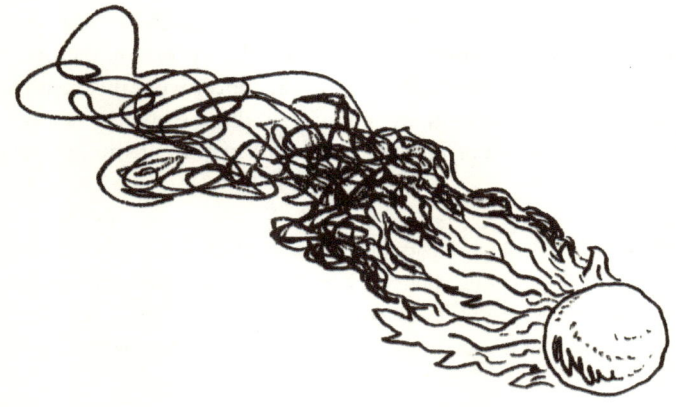

Eight

What would it mean to be drawn into meanings that, in some profound and necessary sense, shatter us?
Christian Wiman (2013)

The Life in the Sky Comes Down Essays, Stories, Essay/Stories

The Fire Says

At six years old, distant enough from the ground to realize that you can connect the closely seen and the far away, the detail and an extension of details, I began the dogging of my father.

The problem remained that Andreas—a name my father preferred to any smaller sound, one he always ordered his single son to use—was so rarely there that the determination to pursue him might be answered by nothing except its own abrupt, kindling charge. Even so, sufficiently removed from the grass that continued to support me, I saw how the long dilemma of my father's scarcity gave out a range of possible solutions.

Leaning against the front door, both feet on the slate walkway that bordered the wide rectangle of the lawn, I spotted one of those solutions in the form of a trail, whose contours I started to trace around the cherry tree, strangely de-petalled by the thicket of storms burring village and sky together, all that May. I accompanied it up, over the rock garden, while it seemed to slow in the willow's stooping green; I noticed its golden rippling; I thought I could smell the ghosts of my father's cigarettes and hair cream, as though the ripples were exhaling. Unaware if the ghostly were capable of exhalation, I resumed following the trail into the backyard, through the screen door, past the denim shirt I imagined to be growing, somehow, out of the stone floor beneath it. I discovered myself in the bedroom that my mother had left to Andreas a year ago, when I overheard her saying that she was going to live with another director who would give her face the exposure it deserves—and will repay. Because I didn't know how to seek for her, I obeyed the obligation to accept her loss. Standing over the bed, undone, finding the trail's collected stuff in my hands, a near yarn of hair that my father's head declined to go on pushing out, I understood how you can hunt for a man in need of reassembly and still not spy him, summoned, on the other side of that effort.

I wondered what it would mean to carry on trying.

It meant, this struggle over time to amass indications of my father's presence, not that Andreas should be restored to perfect wholeness by virtue of their gift but that he'd been there at all, memorialized by a son adept at gathering the tokens of him together. I arranged them in little heaps in places where Andreas would be sure to see them—on his pillow, on the toilet lid in his bathroom, on the computer in the study. I came to understand that these repeated accumulations assumed an Andreas who would lose a button, for instance, along with the boy who committed himself to returning it to him, exchanges which could only confirm the two identities engaged in them. This was before the imperative that seemed to descend on me, requiring me to hold tight even to those remnants of Andreas that others would call impalpable.

I stood in the driveway, just after Andreas and a butter-colored woman had propelled the red convertible into it. They vanished behind the study door. I was listening to the engine's heat as it aimed through air in a lengthening rumble, my right hand straining over the hood to concentrate its upsurge, cupped inside my palm. But the front door thumped, and Anna, the woman with whom Andreas intended to replace a mother gone elsewhere, at least in terms of meals and housework, was maintaining that you couldn't keep what must always disappear. While she spoke, I knew that the car's heat, having poked through skin, was moving in a wave up my arm; I identified Andreas as its source; I knew that its intensity would be mine, for the brief time that my flesh might contain it. Perhaps that was what they were for, the buttery-haired woman lying with Andreas on the study's sofa, or the Anna who sometimes swayed underneath Andreas in her room off the kitchen: meant to stoke a fire of blood and bone until it vaporized into breath, which you can't keep. Anna went on talking about dinner, about bedtime. I felt myself watching the memory of a late night moment in which Andreas, hesitating in the doorway, a grooved **V** between his eyes, looked hard at the son he took to be in bed, asleep. I memorized that look.

Through the distance between us, it taught me that the father didn't know what the son was for.

Two years later, Anna informed me, according to Andreas and his instructions, that I might visit the Long Island City studio, if my attendance verged on the invisible. From the first of those visits, I recognized how you can speak well of distances, since the sighted see, the unsighted move, because of them. The crew busied themselves in setting up a shot in which a woman with cropped, almost jagged hair was staked among hurling flames. They popped; they hissed; yet she made no sound. Her scorching was meant to multiply the sales of ice cream throughout the country, I later learned, as if the sudden cut to a creamy squall, frozen in some cardboard tub, could release her from the leaping yellow, douse her. But she'd never be put out.

She'd go on flaming.

From where I waited, among shadows at the rear of the sound stage, I was about to sense something wheeze and slide as it shouldered a weight that it didn't choose to carry. What I'll soon know to call a dolly had the camera and its operator on top of it, the whole angled diagonally towards the woman who remained on fire, stopping short of the flames themselves, leaving a space that would equal the length of Andreas, if he could be laid on air and hover five feet off the ground. Stepping in closer, pausing just below the cameraman's back, I watched the monitor, whose image focused on the woman's head, on her pupils, inside which burning jumped and bobbed, the gap between camera and woman flattened out, rubbed out, wiped away, though that interval allowed this picture to be born and to lie about its birth. Beyond the monitor, opposite the cameraman, Andreas detached himself from scolding the woman to hold her face so that the light could leap across it: he was staring at the boy who'd come too near and above whom a klieg-lamp fizzed, warning me to re-angle the direction of my eyes.

Afterwards, many years afterwards, it will seem that I saw the figure of a man whose hair retreated quickly from the sternness of the face beneath it. But, in that moment, the baking gulf between father and son guided me to see that I would burn.

And the burning must mean that you were found.

The Life in the Sky Comes Down Essays, Stories, Essay/Stories

Nine

The Life in the Sky Comes Down Essays, Stories, Essay/Stories

Wanting

Dr. Siegel says *You've tested negative*, and you imagine that the hook hidden in his mouth pierces through each word: his bottom lip sticks against his teeth on *negative*, as though he could hardly bear to let it go. But Dr. Siegel's like that, with words.

    You remember—when you came before—the particular kind of quiet with which he met your nodding at his Harvard and Columbia degrees, while the swimming pool trembled through the slatted blinds. You recall the way he withdrew the needle from your arm: slowly, as if he wouldn't let it go. Now, you see Dr. Siegel offer you his hand, hear him praise your *luck*, as Mrs. Siegel waves from the pool still visible through the window. Once she appears in the office, you greet her as a longtime friend of the family, and she takes your hand. You remember the time before, when you tried to shake Dr. Siegel's hand; he removed it quickly: he could only let it go.

    As you walk through the waiting-room on your way to the car, you're trying to notice the U of the receptionist's smile, the copies of *Ladies' Home Journal*, in which recipes for casseroles and cookies must sit, waiting to be used. You're not going to recall the last time you saw Derek in the hospital, when you attempted to feed him some translucent broth from a little spoon. You didn't recognize his mouth. Underneath the sheets, his legs were swallowed by the bed. You wiped the broth that ran down his chin. You felt the bone there.

•

Driving home, you take Town Road because it cuts through the rye fields, where you can see the few houses hunched under a sky that won't go away. When you make the left turn too fast, crows fly low, out of the rye—they brush against the windshield. You could have hit them.

    You can't want to be back with Derek for the last time that you remember him walking. You can't want the rye to be long and green and glimmering, as it was when you struggled to follow the footpath around the fields. Derek's left hand hung from your shoulder: walking, he slid his feet across the ground.

No farther, he said.

•

You park the car, approach the house, and are about to unlock the sliding front door when you find your face reflected in the glass; it arrived there before you. Through that face, you spy the coffee mug in the dish-drainer, the plate on the kitchen-counter, the linoleum floor under the four coats of wax that you gave it last night, since you couldn't sleep.

When you couldn't sleep, you used to sneak downstairs and sit at the kitchen table. You'd hear Derek's feet on the floor, feel him curve his lips around one of your ears: the last time, he simply stood there before you, almost murmuring—*I've been tested*.

Through his pajamas, his legs gleamed, thick with hair and veins. They seemed to rise out of the ground.

•

After you take off your clothes in the bedroom, you look at the negative of your body in the mirror, at the road of chest hair traveling down to the crotch, at the taut thighs between which your cock stands, without the ability to remember. The hair on your calves forgets him; it grows without thought. You think you want to say—*I don't know how to live*. You try to say it.

And you can't.

Ten

The Life in the Sky Comes Down Essays, Stories, Essay/Stories

Figuring Images (2)

I've been thinking for a while of a still life by Cézanne, his *Pommes* of 1878-1882. In Paris, John Maynard Keynes bought the picture "on his own behalf" after purchasing, for the National Gallery, nineteen works from the Degas collection in March 1918, and Quentin Bell reports, many years later, the painting's tale of disembarkation in "A Cézanne in the Hedge."

On the evening of 28 March, "deposited" on the "walk up to Charleston," Keynes stood the Cézanne in a "hedge surmounting a ditch," where it remained, due to an abundance of "luggage" which Keynes couldn't "manage," outside the home of Virginia Woolf's sister, Vanessa Bell, until Duncan Grant and David Garnett "rescued" it after dinner. We can now find it on loan to the Fitzwilliam Museum, Cambridge.

There, we discover what Woolf terms, in her 1918 *Diary*, "the 6 apples in the Cézanne picture," whose coloration ripens "redder" and "rounder" and "greener" under the duration of our looking. Because the picture merits my hanging on its clustered luminosity, I opt not to address at any length Woolf's troubled numeration. But I ponder how she amends the defect of her numeracy by delivering to us, thirteen years on, in *The Waves*, six individuals circling round a Percival whose presence they and Woolf's readers can palpate, yet whose voice is denied us, just as we're refused the identity of the novel's narrator but for the typographical indices that she was there. Like Percival, the narrator's quotation-marks, as they frame these six friends' musing speeches, redouble a superaddition to the visuality that can't quite be accounted for, even as the book represents it, this inability on our part to explain, to reckon, to reason out with sufficient exhaustiveness. Though the Cézanne yields seven, not six, apples, with Woolf, we might ask: "what can" such "apples *not* be"?

The world, of which apples here resemble figurative shards, won't be exhausted or drained away by the precept that it should defer to our explanations of it. Alongside Woolf, we can "wonder" whether the roundness, the rubicundity of these fruit (scrabbled with green) is meant to reference Atalanta's mythic course to a marriage she imagined avoidable, to memorialize and multiply the beauty, then plumply golden, that she couldn't withstand plucking from the ground. Or are Cézanne's apples, in their curvaceous plenty, descriptors of the amatory exertions incumbent on our desire to realize what personhood prescribes for us, the admittance, as Simone Weil formulates it in her *Cahiers*, that to labor is to feel with our whole selves the existence of the world, that to love is to feel with our whole selves "l'existence d'un autre"? If we see the painting subject to the radiance of this latter vision, its apples become visual synonyms both for the persons realized through their adherence to the twofold covenant of laboring and loving and for the bounty that adherence produces. Its maker's apples visualize more than an intensified "we are," given that, unlike Eve ensnared in the circuit of her ecstasy, we can't choose to eat them: they endure the strain of our eyes. And it's the conception of "ecstasy" that takes me to Woolf's "A Sketch of the Past" in her *Moments of Being*, because the pedagogy of the shock which attends it coaches us for what it is to look and for who may be said to do the looking.

My scrutiny starts with an examination of Woolf's title, the limen through which we enter the "little platform of present time" that slides "over the depths of the past." Already, however, we arrive at a temporal platform—undulant, liquefied—as difficult to divine as the "invisible presences" whose "depths" uphold it. To sketch the "impression," the pressing in, the bearing down, of such upholding is to understand its recorder (the "person to whom things happened") as the deputy of "any human being" who endeavors to study, from the guardhouse of the moment, a past that diverges from and sustains his look-out. I see Woolf's textual industry as representative of her readers' dilemma, to the extent that those readers militate against failing to allow for the toilsomeness of gazing back at what seems so gone from them. As I concentrate on all that Woolf's title connotes, the sketch—in its preliminariness, in its accepting the irresolvable through never being finished—qualifies the past as it images a depth, an entirety, it can't compute. In this sense, Woolf apprehends "relation" to mean the angle at which we picture a totality beyond our power to measure within the boundaries of any frame, implying that our vigilance lies in accounting for the space that angularity posits. Any picture angles us towards what it can't enclose and is, by definition, fragmentary, a definition that it's our human business to recollect. But what of the person engaged in recollection? How can we characterize her?

I adjoin two ideas, that of the expanse posited by the angular and of the being put beyond, pushed outside, the precincts of the sensory, which "ecstasy" appears to impose on us, so that under the force of ecstatic experience, we're as though withdrawn to the breadth that we could never decisively represent. But Woolf sketches both the extra-sensory, the being ousted from the sphere of the senses, and the memory that musters its refluent "impression": the "firstness" of her mother sitting "in a train" while it speeds on to Cornwall, of lying "on her lap" and therefore seeing the "flowers she was wearing very close," though this "firstness" is challenged by:

If life has a base that it stands upon, if it is a bowl that one fills and fills—then my bowl without a doubt stands upon this memory. It is of lying half asleep, half awake, in bed in the nursery in St. Ives. It is of hearing the waves breaking, one, two, one, two, and sending a splash of water over the beach; and then breaking, one, two, one, two, behind a yellow blind. It is of hearing the blind draw its little acorn across the floor as the wind blew the blind out. It is of lying and hearing this splash and seeing this light, and feeling, it is almost impossible that I should be here; of feeling the purest ecstasy I can conceive.

Given the bifurcated nature of "the first memory," forked by "red and purple flowers" on the "black ground" of her "mother's dress" and by the metamorphic enterprise of the above passage, Woolf exhibits that to "begin" by visualizing the inaugural image is to spawn a plurality of images. There will always be more than one picture assignable to our own beginnings, meaning that incipience occurs within a continuity, inside an "immense . . . force of life" from which each thinking body emerges and into which each is born. Inauguration points to our envelopment in a continuousness inescapably antecedent to us, to which our relation must be prepositional, intransitive, indirect, indicating that the pictures through which we describe our experience are always at an angle to what they could never orbit round. Because many of us (often) equalize "picture," "relation," and "world," the impossibility of the orbital image can only be understood as a failure to which we should capitulate. But, for Woolf, the capitulation to the "impossible" may be cast in different terms, regardless of those terms' nearness to contradiction.

I say "contradiction" since, if we consider the "ecstasy" that Woolf impresses upon us, we confront opposing systems of discourse and of the self that resorts to them. Woolf's recourse to depicting "ecstasy"—the delight that heaves us away from the body, though the latter springboards us into exaltation—propels its account to the verge of the ineffable. To heed the words shut in the mouth of the past, to regain the experiential images described by those words, to lever up the body: Woolf devotes herself to an *eidolopoeia*, to a form-making, which, while it cranes towards the inexpressible, must be grasped in accordance with some communicable foundation. If the past is never silent, if it murmurs in the ears of the present, that past, with respect to its listener's notational exertions, assents to communication and its exigencies. Taking such a past, however, as one name for what outdoes exhaustive description, we find how the supra-discursive reaches a settlement with what it's possible for us to say, how to render that settlement (that speaking picture) with patience and distinction is to motion towards its very impossibility. And, in this manner, Woolf's use of the conditional guides us in our reading.

When turning to the logic of if/then, Woolf hypothesizes all that follows from it. She administers, within the category of metaphor, the metonymic transfer of "life" to "base" and "bowl," as though tendering an understructure clarified, in a limpid light, the trough both additively filled and disposed to further transmittal. But, here, pattern performs the work of light: it beams at the sequence that ramifies from a framework beneath which it can't probe. That incapability of probing reflects the character of the target, missed, the aim, evaded—and rebounds on the writer whose sentences traverse a vigor they can't "explain." Such is the seemliness of Woolf's "if" as it measures out a sentential series, each prefaced with an "it is" that conveys the memorial weight carried by the whole. The benefit of "lying" between sleep and wakefulness, between inside and out, becomes the recognition that their abutment is porous, there in the room where the sea breaches walls while it breaks on sand. Through the conditionality that orders her descriptions, the self seems "one" and "two," an antiphon to the liquid rhythm "behind" and before the "yellow blind," since "lying," "hearing," and "seeing" broadcast an accord as "impossible" as the "I" who apportions and is pervaded by it. "Ecstasy" designates a pervasion in which the senses are seized, only to be escaped from. We can avow that seizing. But to retail our escape is to hazard the threshold of what, with Woolf, we can "conceive" though not altogether say.

Yet Woolf's "next memory" broaches another sort of seizure:

It still makes me feel warm; as if everything were ripe; humming; sunny; smelling so many smells at once; and all making a whole that even now makes me stop—as I stopped then going down to the beach; I stopped at the top to look down at the gardens. They were sunk beneath the road. The apples were on a level with one's head. The garden gave off a murmur of bees; the apples were red and gold; there were also pink flowers; and grey and silver leaves. The buzz, the croon, the smell, all seemed to press voluptuously against some membrane; not to burst it; but to hum round one such a complete rapture of pleasure that I stopped, smelt; looked. But again I cannot describe that rapture. It was rapture rather than ecstasy.

The Latinity underpinning "rapture" levels our attention at a stoppage triggered by an onrush of the sensory, this passage showing the self's transfixion before a "whole" that voids motility as a proof of its duress. The young girl of "August 1890" and her author are transported to a "stop," a halt, a desisting from withdrawal, whose effects may be listed by reference to how they strum on human skin, ear, nose, and eye, though a total articulation of their phenomenal and emotive cause will elude any catalogue. The perceptible superabounds with an ebullience comparable to that of its receptor, as the latter is both suspended in her veinous skin and lexically diversified. And superabundance warrants a "stop" put to the progress of our reading, signals the question, what is this selfhood that boils over, that redoubles its representations?

Combined, the two passages forward our harking to the primacy of a sumptuous awareness, as if the hospitable "bowl" of the body were a satellite dish, a basin for the reception of impulses actuated by a "life" that stood always outside transmissive instrumentality. The first passage positions its "I" in the vicinity of the "impossible"; the second couples determinate personhood with a "one," generalized because of its global individuality, abstract because the "hum" that spirals "round" it draws a course which words "cannot" dispatch. But the "one" who deploys them can, by their use, discriminate "rapture" from "ecstasy," differentiate between the being riveted to sensation and boosted beyond the body's ambit—and such activities, correlative due to their dispensing "one," are encrypted in the semicolon usage so prevailing in the second excerpt. As semicolons punctuate a series of verbal materials whose members require internal commas; as they station, within the flexure of the sentence, independent clauses not linked by coordinating conjunctions, they arbitrate between organ and body, distribute part to "whole," and spring back on their distributor. Intermediate between the mind's moving forward and the attainment of an idea's full "stop," they also notate the intake of air essential to the long exhalation of a sentence and, with regard to clauses, witness correspondences they don't elucidate. As such, they make a gift to us of the elucidating act.

Leashing together all these significations, we find how the passage mounts variants of them on the page: sentences one, four, and five recruit the semicolon to demarcate successive elements, both phrasal and participial, devised to qualify what it is to "feel" when seized by the current of the observed. Their combined constituents should aid us in ascertaining the properties of the pronoun—or, in the case of sentence four, those of the scene—they modify. Yet combination posits a "whole" that mathematics won't award us.

Woolf's unconventional semicolon usage, her string of participles and incomplete clauses, tells us that here we meet with the myopia of an eye fixed on the part. Since linguistic indicators of personhood, sometimes discrete, sometimes multiplying discreteness, parallel the treatment of the seen, the ways in which its concatenated units "stop" on the page before the "whole" they surmise, its pieces sieved by the senses of touch, sound, sight, we are countenanced in taking the categories of person and environment as counterparts of wholes, abstract in so far as both seem deducted from, and summaries of, ever more voluminous entireties.

Thinking later of her father, Woolf will commend to us the dual abstraction I'm propounding: she culls "from a whole single qualities" which form "part of that whole," the "whole" being "different from the qualities" of which it's "made." If any depiction ratifies its referents, however notionally, infelicitously, Woolf's culling obliges us to tarry in our study of abstraction and its purposes. I rephrase my earlier questions: who are these persons insusceptible to the arithmetic of their "qualities"?

Before making a rejoinder to that query and discussing what Woolf dubs the "ancestral," those "exceptional moments" magnified by the "sledge-hammer" thumping of their "blow[s]," I enlarge upon the commonplace wisdom which construes the abstract in antithesis to the real and which utilizes opposition as a taxonomic principle. My taxonomies at once allude to the substantives they invoke and to our propensity for depicting them—to the enigmatic "conception" laboriously limned, to the thing behind or ahead of us in the space whose scale cedes us the benediction of movement. But if to think the concept is to commit it to becoming an apprehensible thing; if to think the object is to seal it in thought, in thought's classifying concerns, the antagonism so habitually stressed appears predisposed to dissolution. We're parties to this undoing because of the certainty that concepts aren't things, though we beget the latter by means of them, that our creations overtake their makers when, disregarding the process of their begetting, we reconceptualize them as adherents of the ground, as heirs of a nature authenticated by a radiance which won't be "stopped." Such rethinking can, of course, function inversely: we may confound the organic object with the "conception" by whose agency we order it, so that—suborned by the play of a "force" which oppugns our possession and by which we are quickened—object and "force" are remade as simply *ours*. Regarding these fabulations and their consequences in the veridical world, Woolf's approach to the "picture" will assist us in adjudicating the concord or the dissonance between abstraction and what we girdle round with the term "reality"— and in realizing how adjudication submits to "paint."

If she "were a painter," Woolf would stain her "first impressions in pale yellow, silver, and green," their federation seeping "blind," "sea," and "passion flowers" on canvas. She "should make a picture that was globular" in its semi-transparency; "should make a picture of curved petals" and "shells," of "things that were semi-transparent"; she "should make curved shapes showing the light through, but not giving a clear outline." And "everything would be large and dim": "what was seen would at the same time be heard; sounds would come through this petal or leaf—sounds indistinguishable from sights." Woolf brakes the fluency of her image-making when she remarks, farther on, that "picture" is "not the right word" for what flows from it: the ocular and the auditory, "so much mixed," counsel us that we follow a synaesthetic "whole" which the conditional brush couldn't impart to us and which a conjurer of words "cannot describe" in the present indicative available to her. Though "what makes all images too static" is their being steeped in the fixity of their surfaces, their misapprehending what we "cannot analyse" slants us in the direction of the "indescribable," so that the abstract and the real—the palpability of "paint," of canvas, of words on the page—seem inclined to run "together."

I listen to the anaphoric pulse of Woolf's "first impressions," to the way in which receptive insistence marks what it can't enumerate, the "many other than human forces" endlessly "at work on us." I think of Iris Murdoch who testifies, in "Art Is the Imitation of Nature" from her *Existentialists and Mystics*, that "abstract paintings," their objects "dissolving into something else," aren't mere "idle daubs or scrawls, forms wandering round at random in spaces"; they tilt towards "light," "colour," "space," their makers residing "not in a state of total freedom" but "relating" themselves "to something else," to the "world where we normally take colours to be parts of objects." Yet what can be said of personhood as it dissolves into that "something else"?

Up to this point, we've sifted through the incarnations of images from which time has been absented, the "movement and change" attributable to "one of the invisible presences" which tug us "this way and that" and which "position" us, preserve us in a meshwork of dynamics greater than, in the case of time, our globe's axial revolutions around a burning orb. Whether by the lip of a figurative "bowl" or by membranous tissue, the Woolfian self envisaged here conceives a twofold curb, that of a "life" measured by the "container" of its vessel and of an outside that can't quite get in, without exposure to the subjection of measurement. But the limitation inherent in these pictures answers to their virtue and to their poverty: human lives overleap and are overleapt by their representations, the self isn't all, and I recall the "no way out" that James Hillman associates with myth in his *A Terrible Love of War*, even as "A Sketch of the Past" institutes a different set of images for what it might mean to brave the butt intrinsic to a phrase so removed from a "state of total freedom."

The intervals in the "nursery," in the "garden" among the "hum of bees," may induce astonishment at the self's "impossibility," at a feeling inimical to narration in the explanatory sense. Such intervals may look to Hillman's understanding of the mythic as "meaning without explanation," initiate discernment of the "unreasonable," though their pertinence to the idea of others and to a life "lived in common" remains uncertain. But the imagistic collection subsequent to them convokes the intractable, nearly "unveiled," "intensified" by the "sudden shocks" at all that Woolf and those who read her can't "pass" or "escape," illustrating that the impassable constitutes much of what we live "in common." Abstract because of our difficulty in grasping it, the impassable is akin to "reality," just as Woolf's predicaments typify our own.

Suicide, a sometime impotence inside the shadow of a lunging fist, and sexual molestation shouldn't be unknown to us. As human possibilities, they remain at least parts of the imaginable world. Whether as probability or as fact, they wrest from us our admission of what will brook no denial and are "ancestral" since, together, they comprise a portion of our inheritance with respect to how our species moulds time, shapes time, crafts time as though its periodic pattern were "stuff"—and merely ours. Seen in this last light, each of the above actions becomes a vestige of the mythic, given that each is instigated by the dominion of a human hand replicating, in diminished form, the "unreasonable" there seems "no way out" of. But, picturing these actions, Woolf wants us to reexamine our need to extrapolate from the particular to the generalized, to assess the ways in which extrapolation impugns our putative individuality. Thanks to the calculus essential to extrapolation, to how mind speeds along thought and its embranchments, Woolf fuses the "suicide" of "Mr Valpy," a Cornwall neighbor, with the "apple tree," whose "grey-green" bark swells at once with maturation and resultant decay, networking man and tree due to their filiation from a common "force." She recalls "fighting" with her brother "on the lawn": while observing the impulse to "hurt another person" in a "trance" of apperception, the girl she was expanded into a "person" who revoked the principle that punch should retort upon punch, even as her fallen fist "let" her brother "beat her." Yet if velocity of mind projects a thought forward, it can also move by retrogression, figuring an occurrence against the backdrop of its origins.

What shadows these events, what precedes them, reveals a retrograde line of reasoning and remonstrates that our singularity is a lie.

"There," on the "slab outside the dining room door," Woolf's adult half-brother begins to "explore" the "body" of his still young sibling. He digs down "under" the "clothes" into "certain parts" which "must not be touched." The sense that "it is wrong to allow" them to be fingered "must be instinctive," inborn, of an agedness greater than the duration discoverable in the girl "stiffened" on a "slab." But if instinct, in its priority, "proves that Virginia Stephen was not born on the 25th of January 1882," such a confederacy of the instinctual "proves" that her readers join her in being "born many thousands of years ago," that we had "from the very first to encounter instincts already acquired by thousands of ancestresses in the past," that the self is backlit by its antecedents. I am an otherness amid what I think I know, a plurality that predates myself, and everything I seem to have is not mine, but theirs.

All this the "shock" of the outside coming in makes "real" for me—and for the "us" I am.

The Life in the Sky Comes Down Essays, Stories, Essay/Stories

Eleven

The Life in the Sky Comes Down Essays, Stories, Essay/Stories

The Measuring Hour

Our Aunt Fanny began her measuring that summer while dusk stood outside her bedroom windows, preparing to stoop and slide through the screens. She was our father's maternal cousin, daughter of *Senator Joe B*, as our grandmother cared to call him, because of the way he clunked ice cubes in whiskeys too fine for the cold, whose prodigality outdid any counting. Because of his swizzling drinks in the senate in lieu of voting, because of how he'd gossip with his nearby confrères over who was doing what to whom and how precisely muscular was the doing, because of the young man not far enough from boyhood, housed in one of Washington's plushy hotels, the sheets primed for the twining of limbs, the sweat, the slurp of kisses, *Senator Joe B* remained the scourge of our grandmother's fondness for the upright family story. But Fanny's mother was a wonder. Martine, the multiply great-granddaughter of Jules Verne, rose up under the arches of the familial chateau in Nantes, which she held on to for her husband so that he would know where to come back to, even though his extra-marital exertions summoned him always elsewhere. There, she lived with her children, until the lure of New York parties required Fanny's shining in them. Long before that exit, *a kind of widowing*, she mourned, Martine insisted to her son, to her daughter, that she yearned to be Captain Nemo, his submarine fleeting through water as though sea were air. Fanny spelled out these tales at her mirrored bedside table, slowly pulling a wooden ruler from one of the pockets of the robe she wore before dressing for dinner and for Drew, her second husband, who was late. Their house, in northern Westchester County, was surrounded by trees busy with almost talking, crinkled by wind that never stopped. She told my younger brother, Michael, and me how, for the people native to this place, under their feathers, bone necklaces, their tinted skin, *Chappaqua* was the domain of endless rustling, of leaves rattled by gusts, by booming currents. We heard them as she took the ruler out, into the winking light, angled it at her children, Fiona and Ian, at Michael and me, in order to assess the length of our lashes. Fanny said you could surely watch those lashes while they grew—if you looked.

To us, Fanny was a watcher who saw at once where she'd been, where she was, where she couldn't quite be. She was the woman with cone-sized curlers in her hair, a crimson freshly matted on her lips, tending to her girlfriend Patsy's boys, while Stephen, their father, batted balls in tennis tournaments along the curb of the east coast, free from selling television-plugs for products that no one needed, in the little summer sabbatical he'd been given, as Patsy tried not to look at the hiatus she was afraid of understanding. Fanny saw him at the end of an ordinary Madison Avenue day, its racket receding from his armchair in their Upper Nyack house that spread around him, the Hudson lapping on, beyond where the window he was looking through couldn't go. Stephen soaked his head nightly in a fifth of Dewar's, wanting it all to be fuzzed away. A younger cousin at his wedding, Fanny had been the bridesmaid who snipped her dress into an off-the-shoulder gown, one gardenia blooming at her cleavage. She'd been the daughter who married a Swiss aristocrat, Gustav, so cash-poor and beautiful that to gawk at him was to inhale, without end. She saw him on his skis, awhoosh, thumping over snow, saw the adolescent boy he paid for with her father's money on the many weekends he took from her, the boy's neck bruised by a fall that pointed a spotlight on everything, making room for Drew. He appeared in the doorway, asking his children, asking us, when dinner would be available, as if Fanny weren't there, holding her curlers high. We seemed to hear her say that:

Just before our marriage, Drew and I sit on an outcrop in Bear Mountain park that juts over the water, each ripple frozen in an upcurl, the pines behind us yawning from a growl of wind. We watch a blackening downriver thud our way, a tempest that I hope won't be snow, tugging me back to that boy with the ruptured neck, whom Gustav still struggles to keep alive. The ground under us rumbles as the storm lumbers close, and Drew jerks me against his crotch, his head nudging at the hair on my shoulders, my face turned to the sloping shudder above the Hudson. I met him on Patsy's Wainscott beach, on a day hotter than the curries I know he loves. Floating far out, I hear him bob at my side, feel his hand in the hollow of my back, his heat streaking down my calves, my legs all fin, their uplift slowed by the surety of his remaking. Here, lightning crackles through the sky, and rain pounces on the river, its ice parted, opened, as if called. You can hear the crack and ping of it in every flailing pine and shiny rock, steamed by rain that said no to snow.

Drew swings me in a backwards flip, nips up my skirt, pulls at my leggings, and drinks from the cistern between my legs that he knew I was. I see us years after, the multiple divorces, the drinker and the woman who wouldn't again be drunk, because the drinking outpaced anything that she could gauge, because the capacity to gauge told her where she was.

With Drew downstairs, waiting for his dinner to arrive, Fanny will complete her measuring, assuring us that Michael and I claim the longest lashes, their tips so fair that she describes them as hairy light. We'll look at Drew working on his roast beef, his mouth too tiny, pink, fringed by a moustache whose darkness jiggles as he chews. Fanny, rising from the table, will watch her husband driving, hours later, up and down Chappaqua's empty streets, trying not to face the marriage he can't imagine mending. Getting in bed, alone, she understands that the four of us are going to escape the house, run to the cemetery a field away, and lying on fallen tombstones, her own and Patsy's children talk of feats involving vampires and bloodied fangs under the swollen moon, as the caretaker's daughter, from her window overlooking all this, shakes out her words to ask: *are you real?* A mockingbird will tune up a medley of voices stolen from other birds. It sings to the dead, to the living, of the few seconds in which their lips will be wrenched apart, whether ready or unready, by music that can't be unsung. Fanny sees Michael dying, some years on, of a cancer that the doctors maintain need not have been fatal, knows that I won't apprehend what the growing means, if cells and their multiplication undo the body that supports them, leaving me in a world where I can only never find him. She gazes at us in our Upper Nyack beds, months from this moment when her head and pillow meet, as we think of pollen shooting across the air in great green cables, that the life in the sky is coming down, while our father stands above us in a wad of dark, raises up his arms, his eyes one red beam, arrowed on our faces. She hears us wanting to ask, *what are you about to measure with your fists?*, but that must be the wrong question. Our father, Fanny will judge, couldn't know how to answer it.

The Life in the Sky Comes Down Essays, Stories, Essay/Stories

Twelve

'Anybody who voluntarily takes an antiviral every day has to have rocks in their heads. . . . There's something to me cowardly about taking Truvada instead of using a condom. You're taking a drug that is poison to you, and it has lessened your energy to fight, to get involved, to do anything.'
Larry Kramer: The New York Times, May 21, 2014.

The Life in the Sky Comes Down Essays, Stories, Essay/Stories

Albino Boy

From the rear-view mirror, my cabbie asks,
Hey, pretty guy, you gotta boyfriend?
I look up, and his eyes flood the mirror's rectangle with a greenish light that belongs to all the storms I waited for in our Rockland County house. Nose stuck to the window. The smell, the rise, and whoosh of air squeezing in through the geometry of the screen. Outside, everything in somersaults, answering to forces it couldn't see.

    I don't say that the laminated taxi license offers me his name, Malik, though he'll murmur the gift of it after the long curve home from west to east to the Little India where I live, just off Lexington Avenue. That will happen on my building's top stair, while I decide whether or not to unlock the front door. Sniffing the musk of him next to me. Hearing the cab below us huff because Malik will have left it running. I'm unsure of the *yes* he thinks he wants from me. On the verge of being certain enough to insist, Malik leans in:
I can fuck you and still call myself a man.
Jostling now against the back seat, not yet clarifying the absent boyfriend he wishes for, I want to tell Malik how I project, how I almost see, his return, every six months, to Karachi, to the village-girl he may have married, say, when she was on the cusp of sixteen. To the three boys she produced for him, who recognize their father simply as *that man who comes back*, the one who speaks too sternly to them in the dark, at bedtime, since he yearns to lie with the near-woman who can't quite know the man she ought to call her husband. I wish to say: Safiyyah, your wife, must know more than you can guess, and she might learn it from the waving way in which the waters of the Arabian Sea lap and lick and exercise care for the land, bolstering it, striving to prop it up, however briefly, ineptly, even if, millennia ago, all this ground was liquid, heaving. On a few late

afternoons, she walks to where the earth ends, while her sister—from the village that Safiyyah continues to feel taut in her bones—watches over the boys, steams their rice. Turning her head, sometimes, to look back, Safiyyah thinks that the land would rather be aflame than become this element that will always be its origin. More than once, during his many home visits, when he comes to her later than she's ever hoped, Safiyyah finds another man's sweat, acrid, dried quickly to a kind of ash, lingering among Malik's chest hair, in his armpits, on the fingertips that he shoves between her teeth. Down below, he pushes into her.

I wish to tell Malik how this preference for burning is the backstory of my

No, no boyfriend

that parts, that hefts his lips to the moist **W** of a smile. That under gym-bulked bodies, under a pharmacological doze, blood transmits a viral charge that will, for so many and for a time, evade the counting. That all the men with whom I've chafed and rubbed fire into fact were outdone by a virus that's its own sort of blazing. Compelled to burnish, spark, and flare, together we chose cinders over re-emplacement in ancestral waters, just as Safiyyah's earth would, if it enacted the capacity to choose. I want to describe for him the ways in which my lovers were fevered, wasted, snuffed out by what their blood could only go on carrying. To confess that I remain here, in the back seat of his cab, due to the democracy of latex, in combination with my seeing, in the flesh of every man edging close, the ashes that must come after. To add that the irony of envisioning death in all of them has allowed me to escape the wasting, virus-free, and fastened me to the living *no* I was unaware of having chosen.

The taxi swerves on to lower Lexington. Malik greets it with a hail. But I'm thinking of the blazes that shot through houses neighboring ours in Upper Nyack, under the shadow of Hook Mountain, one late September, of the vibrant negative that my mother was, when she and her car met me outside the grammar school. She's not going to detail my father's appetite for the woman with saffron-colored hair, his longing for those tributary veins that collect at the seam above her yellow lashes. His noting their duplicates in a whorl around her ankles, so that the skin seems to forecast what he could claim to be his, if he were to eat her. She's not going to indicate that my father would have

abandoned home, wife, child in favor of these alimentary couplings with a personal assistant in his textile firm, had the former not declared:
Wifehood doesn't interest me.
She won't explain that my father stands suspended between the marriage he thought he wanted   and a freedom for which he'll finally be unprepared. Her belly heaped against the steering wheel, she won't present my brother's forthcoming birth as proof that something can be made of suspension.

But she will, on our drive to the Hudson, brake swiftly at a traffic signal, raise her right hand, point through the windshield at what she calls
The albino boy,
whose radiance quivers within the crosswalk. About to combust. To restore him to the sky, this generator of heat and air and late summer fires that appear to torch each roof on either side of us.

I rethink that restoration to the sky before my building's front door. And I unlock it now, while Malik aims his
Take all of me inside you
at my ear. While I touch the meeting place of his lips with my hand. While afternoon sun descends in angled wands between us, invoking the luminescent boy who'd tell me, if he could:
We survive radiating light, without combustion or dispersal, by remembering how the earth that once was water sustains us, its continuity of motion not to be mistaken for standing still, its always moving the Yes we live by, regardless of our ability to support the saying of it.

The Life in the Sky Comes Down Essays, Stories, Essay/Stories

Thirteen

The Life in the Sky Comes Down Essays, Stories, Essay/Stories

Bett Spools It Back

When I think of him, I remember the mirrors in his eyes, where anyone who stood in front of him seemed to live. I was in there for a time, too, off to the side and as if in the middle of moving out. But those mirrors were on his bedroom walls in Montauk, and we met in Amagansett, so let's spool this back: I was pumping gas at the last filling station before Long Island's final slip-sliding into the ocean, below those cliffs with the lighthouse on their backs. I was too old to be called a girl but liked the calling anyway, wearing denim overalls a bit snug for my butt, my name stitched in a blue rectangle just over my right tit. He wheeled up in his Karmann Ghia the color of a pomegranate ripped open, so that you see the pulp and the juice spilling out, its red a little tired of itself, wanting to be purple. I noticed him, first, because of his car, the top hunched down, wriggling in the wind, second, because of how he stared at what he would later say were the laburnum trees, their yellow petals coiling high behind the garage: he saw them as if looking were a way to listen for the jangle they ought to make, flowers in the shape of coins. Third, I knew him for what he was, the man whose music I'd grown my hair to, from when I really was a girl. On his CD covers, hulked over by his cohort with the halo fuzz around his face and the skimpy, candy-colored lips, he was framed in a vanishing he hadn't known he'd longed to pull off. I was playing with the hose, jiggling the nozzle. He asked what happened to the *e* that should end my name. It will be there once I earn it, I said, and he answered that he'd like to help me with what the earning meant. He was watching my hair flit and waggle in the crack between my legs, saying that it reminded him of young mustard blooms he'd seen in France, on tour. He gave me his credit card, said that I could call him Petey, that we should ride out to Montauk tomorrow, when the sun flings itself into the water. I liked that image, and I followed it, for a while.

What happened next I need to slow down, since everything sped up as I looked at it. Inside his car, as we trailed the *S* that Bluff Road makes on its push away from Amagansett, his right knee bumping against my left, his eyes like a windshield full of pictures that came and went, I thought how the beach, the ocean with late sun jumping into every wave, the privet-hedged houses were hurried into motion alongside us, though they stayed in their places, and we kept moving. A demo of a new CD twanged from the back speakers, he was going solo, and wanted to know what it was like for this girl, whose hair stretched past her knees, to pump gas. After college, everyone I knew stood in a carton that contained their lives, busy with one job, one man, one dog, each of them lasting until they stopped. I decided to try not doing for as long as I could stand up to it, to wait for when the not-ness would open out, on to something else. You're the track I follow / even when you're not there, Petey sang from the stereo, a chorus of South African-sounding men whooping behind his broad vowels. We were about to trace the curve around Napeague and its hump-like dunes, where I'd find a heron eyeing the bay, raising its white throat in one gurgle, then a croon, as if that tune could take the sun and shove it, now, below its outspread wings. We were about to drive up the dirt path to his house, all windows on rough grass, hung over the ocean. Everything began there, on the other side of that glass, even if I didn't know what the beginning was.

We walked in under the pale wood tepee of his ceiling, and I was thinking how small Petey was. His toes, sneaker-free, were short, rounded, his fingernails squared off, the hands narrow but wide enough to strum and pluck from those guitars leaning on his dining room wall the songs that waited inside them, in a crowd, to come out. His housekeeper had lit a fire in the bedroom, its flames dipping and spiking against the grate. I heard them pop what he told me were their sixteenth note rhythms over his naked back, over his little ass, over my right hip. The skin warmed under his hand. I watched copies of Bett and Petey move close together on every mirrored wall, on his bed, where his eyes and hair were the color of dried peat, as if predicting his name. When he said that he'd dreamed of us lying here, on the covers, he kissed me like the brother I didn't have. And when he whispered would I be his beard, I was about to say that facial hair didn't interest me, when I saw everything he could be clear of: the demographics pitched to him by his record company, fan clubs wanting him married, kid-versions of himself circling around his calves, or dating an equally famous woman, her gifts just shy of his, allowing her to fit the game and not outplay it. For a few years, I gave him the other way that he asked of me. In camera flares, in bias-cut dresses, I covered the men I mostly didn't see, though I knew they had to be tall, dark-haired, and offer Petey a taking he yearned for. They never stayed long in the elsewhere I put them in my head, and they didn't talk when they should have been quiet. All this became the not doing that showed me how to head out.[5]

In southern Sweden, where the Baltic Sea wraps a y-shaped tail around the coast, I'm the woman who lives in this place because she doesn't know it, who bikes to the village store, buys cheese, flat bread, and beer, riding on to a wide black lake that no one else seems to come to. Dusk starts to settle on the junipers. A buck and his doe nibble at the low berries, their blue like the light that huddles over the water. I'm the woman who never saw that Petey and his demographics were always coupled, even when we were alone in our many rooms, since their coupling made possible the life that was his. I'm in a country where I don't hear his name. But, a few months from this moment, I'll learn that he's married a woman who sings twangy songs that sound like his, if you could listen to them with a single ear. She's about to have his baby, I'll read, though that stays a mystery I won't trouble myself to solve. White moths flap among the junipers, wind bangs and jags their upper branches, and I'm the woman who moved out, who understands that every now escapes especially those who stop enough to recognize it, as it goes, the woman who adds this *e*, finally, to her name.

---

[5] When I was in music school in Boston, Bett would come and stay with my roommate and me on Gainsborough Street, the rows of apartment buildings not yet gentrified by becoming condos. I remember how this story was a weight that she felt urged to carry, alone. But I wanted to carry it with her.

The Life in the Sky Comes Down Essays, Stories, Essay/Stories

Fourteen

The Life in the Sky Comes Down Essays, Stories, Essay/Stories

Figuring Images (3)

What Virginia Woolf describes in "A Sketch of the Past" repays her readers' capacity for hovering over it: there, on the "slab outside the dining room door," Gerald Duckworth, her much older half-brother, begins to "explore" her "body." She is still "very small." He digs down "under" the "clothes," into "certain parts" which "must not be touched"; the sense that "it is wrong to allow" their touching, even when compelled, "must be instinctive," inborn, of an age greater than the duration discoverable in this girl "stiffened" on a "slab." But if instinct, in its priority, "proves that Virginia Stephen was not born on the 25th of January 1882," such a confederacy of the instinctual "proves" that her readers join her in being "born many thousands of years ago," that all of us, in diverse ways, "had from the very first to encounter instincts already acquired by thousands of ancestresses in the past," that the self is backlit by its antecedents. I am otherness amid what I think I know, a plurality which predates myself, and everything I seem to have is not mine, but theirs. All this the "shock" of the outside coming in makes "real" for me—and for the "us" I am.

Or so Woolf would have us think.

Yet to read such moments with sufficient fullness, to detect how they are "connected," we must struggle, always, to reassemble them. Reassembly centralizes our attention on parts tending towards a "whole" which undoes their mere totaling up; it also underscores our participation in what envisioning means, since we'll have remade the "scale," the "scaffolding," by which any human life is upheld, even if it must be more, that life, than the metaphors appendant to it. Our metaphoric profusions, the ways in which we transfer the attributes of one thing to another along a line of likeness, of kinship, nevertheless affect the comportment of our thought together with that of the behaviors conjugated by it—and all

The Life in the Sky Comes Down Essays, Stories, Essay/Stories

dispense the vision we undertake in common. Adapting Thomas Hardy's *Moments of Vision and Miscellaneous Verses*, Woolf neither replaces "vision" with "being" nor conflates the two terms: in its collective significations, "vision" signposts "moments of being" and the "shock" which heralds their advent. To undergo exhumation, to succumb to our unearthing from a tumulus of inattention, to accept that the pictures of our succumbing will always be unfinished: these verb phrases meet in the momentary "being" of sudden sight. But the far-sightedness open to us must be prepared for, equipped with our cognizance of an apprehending eye, mind, and the "shock" which actuates both. However brief the "blow[s]" that enkindle me into "being," I can remember them; out of their sequencing, I initiate a thinking through the irradiation of their images. Doing so, I rally what it was—and will be—to have been.[6]

With Woolf, we can recognize: I irrupt into an outside forever incomplete with respect to me. When my sense-faculties encroach on completeness, on within and without consummated, divisionless under the rush of feeling, my body foils its anticipated union: the almost impossibility "that I should be here" reinstates an "I" inevitably unyoked from a "whole" it can't recover. Enraptured, that "I" may be unable to relate the thoroughness of its arrest, yet it can educate itself in the slow "stop" over the details of the visible and learn not to covet their capture. So far, "shock" names a psyche bruised by where it can't go, what it can't do; such negations nevertheless instruct me that to think calls for things exterior to the thinker, that those things forerun my collisions with an outside whose "horror" it's possible for me to meet. The interiority of mind required for that meeting shows me what thinking can effect, as ascertaining the "suicide" of a "Mr Valpy," of someone else seen by though unknown to me, I struggle my way into watching the moment before declination, speculate on thoughts amassed before a succeeding fall—the world contains nothing but my despair of it, or anything except

---

[6] Much Woolfian scholarship sees the function of ancestral instincts here as indicating a dissolution of the self. But contact with what precedes us need not equal erasure. To say *yes* to that contact, *yes* to the harrowing moment and how it gives rise to sensations older than the present moment, all these movements can amplify the individual self that lives what may be called its own life, to the extent that this self recognizes and uses what it assents to.

my skills in abiding an extent wide enough for a mind that imprints itself on, that excises itself from, a span I don't know how to match. Such speculations, notwithstanding their accuracy or imprecision, demonstrate the imperious belief that loss must be repaired by the spotting of its ocular equivalent, such as "the apple tree" that Woolf links with the death of her Cornwall neighbor. As if human minds were slung together, the one compensating for what the other couldn't persevere in, I revive, remake the lost in the kin I propose for him, an aging tree, a fallen branch, any object fashioned and subverted by time, whose progressive infringement on things is all I grasp of it.

A probable definition of "horror" here, out of so many, is that the lost is not mine. A thing among things, he declines the restoration I ordain for him and the pronouns by which I submit that he was there. In that lies his gift to me, as both he and the world are unequal to my need that they should be requisitioned. But there are other forms of restitution, of revision, and these can be tested under the searchlight of "reason." Furthermore, "reason['s]" practice of parsing out—of resolving—an ensemble into its constituent elements through engrossed cogitation inserts an indefinite hiatus in the midst of action, signalizes the trial of a new "shock"; so that, if the outside will come in by means of a penetrative fiat, I at once suffer that piercing and behold it from a prepositional standpoint, from a mental distance, in order to "explain it."

Of course, to "explain" my penetration is to recast those actions within my reach, as well as that "I" fledged by the mindful interim between itself and the inescapability of its penetrator. There's a yielding which consorts with rejection: when my brother or any other figure hurls himself at me as though to enforce the nuptials of one punch and another, I can—as my fist unclenches, descends to the ground—disdain that enforcement and reclaim the capability of failing to be requisitioned, an aptitude I retain while the pumping volley doesn't stop, since (for my antagonist) I'm solely a shred of matter under the gravity of his will. And if the "instinctive" can be contemplated, its liaison with what uplifts it allows for a reasoning out, a winnowing out, a "revelation of some order" beneath its drift. Even when overmastered, I can think in concert with all that the body appears to tell me.

Yet, in regard to syntax, to its customary organization in the air and on the page, "mind," "body," "I," and "me" are discriminative terms, moored to articles fixed by their severance from one another, whereas my overmastering rejoins the once separable and furthers thought under the aspect of what it is to act. Despoiled of an interiority by a subject whose prodding maintains that inside will replicate out if both are converted into a redundancy of flesh, a void of stuff raided from diverse positions by what must go on looming over it, I am, for my violator, the evacuation he assigns to me. But even under his fingers (those of my half-brother, of his behavioral counterpart), I'm not the lacuna he makes of me nor identical with my despoliation. The incantation of my "resenting, disliking it," however, befogs my capacity for lighting on "the word for so dumb and mixed a feeling," which, because of its dumbness, of its hybridized properties, appears so large, so monumental, that its anteriority subvenes in this very moment when I sit propped on a "slab." I intuit myself, by means of a depredator's hands, of the instincts they smart in me, as a meditative body that retrogresses from effect to cause: since the former outbalances its patent instigation, effect and cause seem preponderated over by prehistories I can't know, he can't know, though one description of duty may be our recognizing how the prehistorical neighbors on us, renders us more populous than two individuals latched to a singular event. We can each temper "feeling" with the cognitive distance fundamental to reasoned, reflective thought, and such a feat will carry us, if we let it, to the intuition of origins whose remoteness seems to belie the lone particularities we understood we were. Yet, lowering my eyes, I see a man who pinpoints his concentration on plundering an integrity already vaporized before he touches it. While his hands—inspectorial, motivated by a hunger more unsparing than its name—dig under my clothes, while a finger starts the slow push in, he perceives neither the psychic footage between himself and his exertions nor what could otherwise have been done with it, how, under the gravitation of desire, he need not have become equivalent to that desire's object. Going in, he finds nothing but himself, a thing mechanized by an autocracy he failed to contemplate and to be responsible for.

    The "shock" of his entry nevertheless goads me to retrace those other "shocks" startling "being" into play: I've lain in a fetal bed between house and sea, among the intercommunion of sound and sight; have stood in a "gummy" film before a world I didn't know how to reach; stirred at the "horror" of a death I couldn't change; rejected a fist pounding out its disregard for that rejection; and, penetrated, I've sat suffused with instincts not simply mine. "Being," however, appears unthinkable without the backdrop of having-been. Tracking the "instinctive" and its derivations back through distinguishable time-scales, through variable circumstances, social conditions, I discern countless bodies compassed by repetitive despoilments. Each pair generalizes impulses animating the assault precedent to it; each re-enacts a primordial moment almost remembered. Going further in my descent, I come to how we begin inside a coherence which each birth dismembers, so that to be born is to look in both directions, behind and ahead of the single parturition detached from a "whole" all the while in contact with it. If this "intuition" is true, it "proves" that though we repeat "ancestral" behaviors, we're individualized according to the degree and manner in which we honor, recollect, the cohesion which backs us and from which we originate; that deliberative thought trained on the instinctual is a form of action; that "one's life is not confined" to the "body," to "what one says and does"; that we live "all the time in relation to certain background rods or conceptions"; that "there is a pattern hid behind the cotton wool," underlying what we may neglect to see. And how we meditate on "relation" will determine the personhood within our imaginable reach.

Such ideas bring Woolf and her readers to what she "might call a philosophy":

at any rate it is a constant idea of mine; that behind the cotton wool is hidden a pattern;
that we—I mean all human beings—are connected with this; that the whole world is a work of art; that we are parts of the work of art. *Hamlet* or a Beethoven quartet is the truth about this vast mass that we call the world. But there is no Shakespeare; there is no Beethoven; certainly and emphatically there is no God; we are the words; we are the music; we are the thing itself.
And I see this when I have a shock.

I want to slacken the pace of the "we" so noteworthy in the above passage, as well as to suggest that the thinking "behind" Woolf's pronoun has an "ancestral" history, that the "truth" she cites counts the multiform among its possibilities.

If "moments of non-being" outnumber those which countercheck them, "shock['s]" foremost strength belongs to how it heaves us into consciousness out of the fuzz of our own stolidity, out of the "nondescript cotton wool" in which each of us is "embedded." Ejected from (ousted from) the humus of our indifference, we wake to an influx into "being," whose plenitude may be thought out while experienced, remembered after its copiousness appears to dwindle, once we revert to the recumbency inherent in our natal soil. Since plenty, recalled, accommodates analysis and what can be born by virtue of it, the spell of "being," however abridged, expands when memory's composing powers remake it, refashion it, set it free in the "work" which materializes our ripeness for fecundation. The importunity of "being" is generative, if we prolong its experience in the mind. But, with her emphasis on the "work of art," does Woolf simply aestheticize its potential maker, notwithstanding the latter's corporate features?

It seems to me that Woolf saves herself from this indictment because of the "horror" she rates so deserving of the lengthened concentration expended on it, a "horror" whose liberality—its abundant fact, which will not be wished away—mentors her acquaintanceship with how many of our human actualities, of which suicide, the clash "on the lawn," and molestation suffice as models, are structured by us, made by us, accessories to those who propagate them. And, giving us "the other face in the glass," Woolf does not retreat from implicating herself in that "horror." Though

it may appear, whether "dream" or authentic event, that the "incident in the looking-glass" imitates Jacques Lacan's insight concerning the specular image in his *Les Complexes familiaux dans la formation de l'individu*, Woolf neither idealizes nor squares herself with the projection shuddering "in the glass," which seemed so different from the young girl she was. Such disavowals measure out a prime lesson: severing itself from the "background" and moving as though "alive," the thing enciphered in the mirror, the "animal" domiciled in the mirror, prefigures Simone de Beauvoir's conceptualizing, in *Le deuxième sexe*, the socially calibrated alterity of the female body and exhibits that any human corpus, like the universal beauty propounded by Simone Weil, for example in *Attente de Dieu*, must be other than our expectations regarding it. I don't dismiss the "relation" of sex to those expectations. I take Woolf's difficulties as paradigmatic of all our own, given that she repudiates glossing the relational as parity by another name, that the patterned subsists on the ground of what fringes it, that mirrored animality mimes in degraded form the otherness of our provenance, that Woolf's "we" expounds our membership in the word. But, if we're "something else," "something" other than our wellhead, the tract stretched between "we" and its source can be expressed reciprocally: our inception must differ from the "human beings" effectuated by it. On account of the prominence granted here to distinction, is it the case that Woolf exalts either of her divisions to a transcendent order? To respond to that question, to illuminate Woolf's use of the first person plural, I move to James Hillman's *A Terrible Love of War* and its engagement with the mythic.

 Hillman disambiguates the mythical and the ways in which that sector pertains to what it's not. When an impasse coerces us into the conviction of there being "no way out," our catapulting "leap of imagination" into "myth" may aid us in seeing the certitude of deadlock with eyes revitalized by myth's "meaning without explanation," since that phrase solicits our attending to a "meaning" beyond "explanation," greater than the intelligibility which sense-making stipulates. As "norms of the unreasonable," however, myths must be in contraposition to the reasonable, to terrestrial "reason" and its performances, the one high above the other due to its altitude, so that the two fields remain in isolation, except for the human "imagination['s]" supplicating "leap." And Hillman implies the unidirectional quality of movement itself: that which excels us, ensphered by its own elevation, abstains from descending to the districts below it—the transcendent won't come down. Yet, if transcendence qualifies all that we entitle by myth, by what refuses to be reasoned away, Woolf, Weil, and Iris Murdoch (for instance) pose how the real and what climbs above it, what lifts above it with respect to eminent rank, join in interplay, in mutual intervention. With them, I advocate that such reciprocity, regardless of its demonstrable truth-value, benefits those who observe it. Unlike Hillman, all three authors speculate on the equivocal nature of the relationship between the mythic and the verifiably tactile. The two will be difficult to scissor up, so interwoven. One advantage of equivocalness rests on its asking those who admit it that they should risk the snags fundamental to reading an ambiguity deserving of decipherment by more than a single light. Risking readers, in acceptance of that ardency, may envisage "relation" as something other than simple opposition or identity, terms that nullify the very concept they purport to define. But Hillman's bounding "leap," sprung into distance, pits myth against its contrary, ensures their antipathy, and forsakes the means by which "imagination" nears on embodied minds in action.

"La source des actions," what Woolf calls, in "Memories of a Working Women's Guild," "the child of the flesh," our imaginative faculty emerges from all that Weil diagnoses, in her notebooks written while in America, under the name of "la souffrance" which inspires "horreur," "le malheur" we endure against our will, seek to escape, beg to be spared. Nevertheless, our attention to it teaches us that to sustain "un choc," this individualized "shock," is to induce an "imagination" disposed to recognize how the asymmetry between the transcendent and the real, which Weil and Woolf don't deny, needn't render their interconnectivity impossible. We participate in that intercommunication, with or without reference to the "shock" acknowledging it and, in company with the things around us, do so according to a common rhythm. The raying out of the sun stores itself in the tree, as Weil reminds us, wood being at once a transformer and conserver, a reservoir of light. We may unite with her in longing for the chlorophyll through which we might feed on luminosity, "comme les arbes," though our suspension in desire ought to trigger the remembrance that each green leaf, each fruit within the circles of our mouths, enacts our capacity for eating the transmuted light by which we remain alive.

Much would follow from these observations, if we were to keep to them. We'd support the claim that diffuse forces enwreathe, saturate the human subject and the thing inert on the path before her, both maintained by intensities beyond all evidence of their sustaining powers. Like Murdoch when she writes of Platonic discourse in "The Fire and the Sun," we'd hold high "our ability to use visual structures to understand non-visual structures," an "ability" central to "explanation in any field," seeing that the "original role" of Plato's Ideas "was not to lead us to some attenuated elsewhere but to show us the real world," the "work" of being here. As a thing, Woolf's "we" is "connected with" that "work" through the mutuality she upturns over the hierarchy implicit in a conventional understanding of transcendence. For, together, the "visual" and the supra-visual extrude the world, as well as what we make of it.

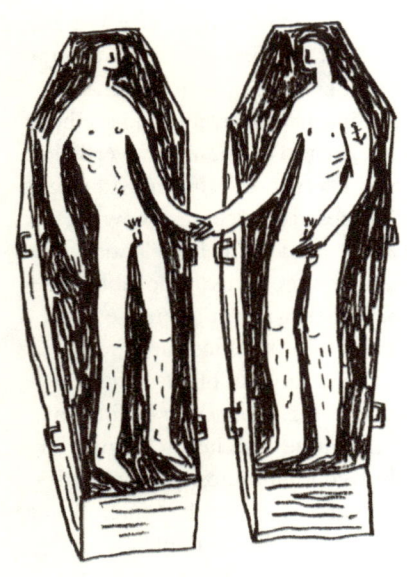

Fifteen

The Life in the Sky Comes Down Essays, Stories, Essay/Stories

Beatrice amid the Rectangles

I want to cross the road in my naked feet. I want to introduce you to Planter's Punch. I want to go on declaring since, as a child, I was forbidden to make a single one, and I have all that time to stand up for.

Beatrice Straight and I were pausing in the middle of Main Street. The whole of East Hampton a welter long after midnight, we saw the magnolia opposite us hoist its throat-colored petals into booming rain, as if to drink must be all. Hitching up her quilted skirt, a shoe in each hand, Beatrice slapped through wet to the other side. A few hours earlier, she was the Jocasta of Howard Moss as he retells the tale in *The Palace at 4 A.M.*, the John Drew Theatre becoming Thebes and Beatrice that body dangling in the window, a half-moon bright as glass over the lake and the mountains beyond its frame. She'd been the woman for whom everything she saw was overtaken by what she couldn't say. Now, from the stoop of 1770 House, its doorway light flicked off, Beatrice shouted that I should follow her, that she knew Niko, who ran the basement bar and who kept it for her, after hours. He'll find you prettier than I can like, but we'll make it go.

At 15, I was an apprentice in Edward Albee's summer repertory company, the playwright recalled—especially—for his ranting couple with the fictive child strangely capable of dying, or at least of being mourned.[7] Our crew hammered sets, rehearsed lines with actors whose

---

[7] I remember, at my audition and interview for apprenticing in Albee's newly formed company, the charged weight of Albee's silence, his staring directly at my eyes. Richard Barr, Albee's company-partner and producer, was charming and appreciative, but I took Albee's never enunciating a word as a cloud over my prospects. I learned later that the staring meant: you merit my attention, and

misremembered words shook sideways on the air. All of us stood in the light of this Beatrice, in her late fifties, so closely resembling her name: she who made happy in particle and wave, the lead in every production that we mounted for Mr. A, as he decreed we should call him, her straw hair flecked as if with bits of raw honey, eyes broad enough for any world to fit there. I found Niko in them while he brought the Planter's Punches that Beatrice paid for, his left hip warm against my shoulder. He smelled like the rain banging at the bar's windows, seeping through panes that dated back to 1663, when the hotel had been a house. Beatrice and I sensed old chronicles encroaching through the vents. You didn't need to talk about them. They were everywhere you could look.

    At the tail-end of the seventeenth century, Niko's basement bar was a kitchen of slop-pails and hooked meats, peopled by the kind that the Long Island newcomers resisted seeing, even as everything above pivoted on the place below. Once their brown, their black bodies slowed at serving, foisted under floorboards, between walls, behind the storage room, accompanied by fragments of the wampum and corn husk dolls that those above stairs failed to value, they were made to brace the house that had rebuked them, though they powered the way it ran. Beneath her bare toes, Beatrice and I heard the murmuring.

    We didn't talk of Mr. A and his Montauk estate, clumped on high dunes too frail for the weight they were forced to bear. We didn't talk about Niko renting himself out at parties under what Mr. A pinpointed as his portico, though the loan, we must have guessed, involved more grappling than Niko planned for. We chose to bypass the subject of a young Christopher Walken, his hair growing thickly in golden bundles if you watched, his Oedipus a Theban king, however betroubled, wedded to the thwack and wallop of bubble gum chomping, nightly. He'd stick it on the throne at center stage, a gift that Beatrice, his multiply familial queen, couldn't coax him out of giving, to which Mr. A offered a silence, sacred, unyielding, like some misdirected vow. We avoided the topic of Moss pacing the area just inside the theatre doors, at each performance trailed by his whispering of the words he didn't know how to lose. I wanted to tell Beatrice that I had denied my

---

attention, earned, has no need of words. The eyes meeting should be enough.

father's fist and was living, too soon, with a woman whose love I mistook for safety. That behind this safety moved all the men I'd chosen before her, in a space populated by longings I didn't know how to judge or not to answer. But, finding a pen in her skirt pocket, across our paper tablecloth, over every red and blue gingham square, Beatrice began to write what she called one of her rectangular stories, about how taking and mistaking always seem to fuse:

    She's the four year old in a poplin dress whose mother, Dorothy, stands tall as a cloud, so that bending down, Dorothy brings a whiff of sky with her. This little girl, with the honeydew eyes, her chin a pointy V, a line under her lower lip to remind her that talking is only what you do when prodded, knows how her mother's name means the gift of gods, the donation from what you can't see to the world that is. She knows that Dorothy huddles in the doorway with uniformed men, their hats like wings, their whispers like the breaking open of a tiny box to discover the prize of words inside it. She knows that her father walks somewhere in northern France, that in 1918, the great bunt and blare across the ocean starts to hush, that the ailanthus outside, sounding slightly larger than silence, arrows down its suckers as if being born anew on other ground should be a simple thing. She hears Dorothy read Empedocles to her in the mornings, one finger in the air bobbing the tempo of every line, learns that you can, at times, have been a boy, a bush, a girl, a bird, a fish, small words aiming at bigger things, at the moment when, months from now, she and Dorothy will be waiting on the Dorset coast. They'll sail over ripples to where her father no longer is, upright. She'll be made to comprehend that a viral slide from trench to trench to plain has stuck her father in the earth, from which he may only stand up as something else. The graves, their sun-bleached crosses, are massed on cliffs above water that forever outreaches what her mother calls our geometries. As Dorothy moves closer, the girl will almost find it possible to ask: how can I ever know whose hand I'm holding?

It's forty years after Beatrice finished writing, reviewing the near trident of lines on my right palm, saying that they tell us we once belonged to the sea, incanting Rilkean words about how any arrow, in its momentum, outlasts the string and becomes more than itself, that the outlasting will be something I'd come to. I'm in my Brooklyn apartment half-listening to, but not getting lost in, the hopeless little screen that Leonard Cohen sings of, where too many faces fling out words among images that never slow and let the looker in. Turning, the screen awash with her, I see Beatrice in the last five minutes of the film that won her those many shiny, naked statuettes, the ones meaning: *Network* and its director, Sidney Lumet, give us pictures we know how to read, how to insert into a world that we allow ourselves to recognize, while we tally all the takings. In a navy suit, that scarf an overcareful knot at her neck, Beatrice wholly, briefly, is Louise in her Upper East Side kitchen, not quite eating her lunch, not quite looking at every salad leaf that she fails to eat, waiting for her husband, absent from their bed for days. Max, she knows, is busy with the body of Diana, the programming executive who oversees him at the television station, she who aligns men (they are always men) with their performances, with what they buy, sell, with how they enact the buying and the selling, while Diana moves beyond any method for prediction, changeful like an autumn day, before the sun, at last, goes. When Max returns, dry and red around the mouth, a flare in his eyes, Louise can already plot his words: I leave you for a woman I can't outguess, whose will lingers where her heart ought to pump, who'll puncture me in ways I won't know how to foresee. Shouting that I hurt, I can hurt, I puncture and am punctured, Louise extends to him all the declarations that she never knew how to give, when she loops back to the kitchen, where the late light greens. If the credits' scroll could've been delayed, we'd watch Louise gaze through the window above the sink at synapse after synapse, firing, fretting across the sky, even if that sky has no brain, and these are electric volleys, charging down. But much can come of lightning. Below my kitchen window, a magnolia in the back garden plumps its blooms. The wind twists, thickens. And I know that it's about to rain.

Sixteen

The world is never done with you.
Ellen McLaughlin (lyrics)/Sarah Kirkland Snider (music), Penelope (2010)

The Life in the Sky Comes Down Essays, Stories, Essay/Stories

Loading

If he were a sentence, he'd be weighted with prepositions. They'd mark the things and people he chose, or felt compelled, to carry. With words like *from*, *to*, *over*, *under*, and *across* as harbingers, aimed at what happens just beyond his pronouncing them, all of it would be beautiful. But why?

We've come to the Place des Vosges at late dusk on this mid-June day, just to watch how one thing becomes ballast for another. We see a spread of sky, at two hours before midnight, supported by the square's blue slate roofs, sharply pitched onto the houses below, their red brick uplifted by vaulting arches the pink of fingernails steeped too long in water. All the cobbles freighted over what once was marsh lead us to his face. We're at Ma Bourgogne for the cassis, among outside tables encircling one of the pillars that brace everything above. He and Bryan, his American friend, sit at a table abutting against our own, one that jiggles as if it had a quake inside, jerking to get out. But the jiggling stops when Bryan calls him by his name: Chanh. Soon, we'll overhear his stop/start French and English explain that "Chanh" means the true one under the heavy summer moon, or something like it, though the Laotian's hard to translate. Chanh wants, instead, to talk about the Mekong River, whose banks he traced with his mother sometimes on his back, so that she'd be free of his country's Civil War before Americans and their camouflaged armies came, in the early 1970s, to bomb/brush aside what was already lost. Yet now each of us under every arch looks up at the plane trees listing in the park, around which the brickwork squares itself, a little before the lamplight starts. We're beneath those rooms where Victor Hugo's single surviving daughter, Adèle, as a child in the 1840s, strained at her father's piano in a sway of knee-length black hair, hoping that music might hold the feeling her world could find no use for. And Chanh's about to tell anyone who listens why the boosting up, the heaving across, through air, should be beautiful—however much we've kept that question to ourselves.

For the last few moments, Bryan's been playing a game of solo squash with his *streak au poivre*. But he pauses as Chanh, the verdancy in his eyes deepening in time with the dusk that lengthens into blue, recounts how we're greening things, made for the rising up, the sun-splaying out, the crumple into yellow, when the dirt takes us back. That was what it meant, when Chanh's parents sent him to be schooled at the Sorbonne in the culture they were taught to worship. That was what it meant, when his father, years before bombs crowded the Laotian sky, left everything for Clotilde, the French woman whose name he could hardly say, even as his body sang beneath her weight. That was what it meant, Chanh's scramble from Paris into Laos, smuggled through the Thailand border, while the North Vietnamese stormed his country along the Mekong, along its grasses, and he saved his mother from the place she'd been abandoned to. She cooks, now, in a many-windowed apartment beyond Austerlitz station, weaving mint around her dumplings for the Chanh she points to as another sun, alight in a man's earth-wandering body that she helped to make. Her face shadows over when she thinks of the word-learning inside her son, how it ought to resemble a flaxen thread twined around every cell, impossible to find, to pull out, or to cut, though it's led him only so far as managing a car repair and gas service shop, as if no one could spot signs of the thread her son became. Sunk too deep, they escape the motion of an eye not belonging to a mother. But, for Chanh, this is what it means to travel that distance between the rise and the crumpling back: you can't control the journey's scale, walking under a sun whose heat you'll never own. He relearns that lesson each time he sees his father selling half-smoked cigarettes near any train station he tangles with himself to get to. Once the mayor of Vientiane, the capital city that the French renamed because they could, his father stands at a Paris street corner, unseen by French eyes that hurry past him, because they can. A few moments on, Bryan will want to say that he's come to France, we think, because he doesn't know how to live in his piecemeal country, where the character of one part-like state easily overtakes the whole, where certain human parts are valued above others. He'll recall Douglas, the man he loved with those black irises seeming to bubble in his eyes, how, on his bed in New York Hospital, Douglas is invaded by Kaposi's sarcoma that scalds islands across his

skin, in whose memory Bryan will need to add: it's 1986, the scorching comes, and I don't know how to belong among my fighting kind. Yet something happens before Bryan readies himself for these words. Under the arcades, now lamplit, we watch a gust that takes up strands of hair and dirt and dust and skin-cells cast off as we pay our bill, so that bits of us ascend in a helix above the plane trees. With Chanh, we believe this transport, this moving, must be a part of what we're here for.
(Onechanh Sisattana: 1950-2013)
(Douglas J. Harnden: 1959-1991)[8]

---

8 When Doug died, I was in Denmark, in a bedroom painted the kind of blue that lips turn, meeting too cold air. I didn't know, then, of John Berger's *And Our Faces, My Heart, Brief as Photos*, from 1984. But I can almost follow Berger, now, murmuring to my loved one: "What reconciles me to my own death more than anything else is the image of a place where your bones and mine are buried, thrown, uncovered, together. They are strewn there pell-mell. One of your ribs leans against my skull. A metacarpal of my left hand lies inside your pelvis. (Against my broken ribs your breast like a flower.) The hundred bones of our feet are scattered like gravel. It is strange that this image of our proximity, concerning as it does mere phosphate of calcium, should bestow a sense of peace. Yet it does. With you I can imagine a place where to be phosphate of calcium is enough."

The Life in the Sky Comes Down Essays, Stories, Essay/Stories

Seventeen

The assistant looked at me with an amused, vaguely ironic expression: better not to do than to do, better to meditate than to act, better his astrophysics, the threshold of the Unknowable, than my chemistry, a mess compounded of stenches, explosions, and small futile mysteries.

I thought of another moral, more down to earth and concrete, and I believe that every militant chemist can confirm it: that one must distrust the almost-the-same (sodium is almost the same as potassium, but with sodium [no explosion] would have happened), the practically identical, the approximate, the or-even, all surrogates, and all patchwork. The differences can be small, but they can lead to radically different consequences, like a railroad's switch points; the chemist's trade consists in good part in being aware of these differences, knowing them close up, and foreseeing their effects. And not only the chemist's trade.

Primo Levi: The Periodic Table (1975)

The Life in the Sky Comes Down Essays, Stories, Essay/Stories

Figuring Images (4): Talking to the Dead

In the current American climate, while Donald Trump lunges, successfully, for the White House by ranting from platforms, screens, and newsfeeds against the women, the immigrants, the refugees who must be identical with his contempt for their differences from him, as if a word matched its referent, always without slippage, I talk to the dead. To two long gone, especially: to Virginia Woolf and Plato, their resonances stretched across the millennia separating them. They're tough to hear, those echoes, but the listening can be earned, so long as any hearer balks at the sameness that lives on the other side of Trump's disdain for the differential. Part of our human trade, as Levi sketches out, ought to involve defying the effort to squeeze persons into our vision of them, to batter down two into one, whether or not we're mindful of the consequences of such an act, its potential explosions. Together, Woolf and Plato help their listeners to resist equalizing the seer and the seen, or at least to understand that the consequences of resistance, as well as its failure, are ours.

I remember that a great deal revolves around how we, her readers, think out the principle of "connected[ness]" so preponderant in Woolf's "A Sketch of the Past." To determine that we live "all the time in relation" to constitutional "rods," "conceptions," to a "pattern" lurking "behind the cotton wool" of our experience of the given isn't to decide that what lies beneath triumphs, strangely, over what stands upon it. Encoding the former and the latter in visual vocabulary, Woolf allows for our inference that perhaps both emerge from interdependent derivations. But when she asserts that "one" is "not confined to one's body," to "what one says and does," Woolf fails to produce the consequence that the individual's approach to that which fortifies the visible may be described as straightforward, effortless, tranquil. Since "shock" beckons the seeing of connectedness, to see well is to abide by the pricking pain that enhances what the eye can take. To register that twinge, that enhancement, necessitates a body whose commitment to unstinting vision will affect its conduct inside the "cotton wool" bequeathed to it from birth and within the "pattern" behind that bequest, a correlation accentuated by how Woolf's representative language pleaches together the two nominal phrases as visualizing systems. With linguistic precision, Woolf settles that, for all of us, a wakened access to any spatiality is never direct, never unmitigated, never of limitless duration. And her prepositions throughout her description of that problem, in concert with the nouns they govern, with the verbs whose relational qualities they nuance, steer us towards the variety of connection she judges at once meritorious and real. Whether or not we struggle to perceive with adequate limpidity, so much intervenes between ourselves and the nucleus of our attention: the past as it bridges the present; how we orient ourselves in the direction of the moment; the personhoods evolved across both time-divisions—these collect in interposition while we entrust ourselves to the perceptual act. If a "pattern" conceals itself "behind" the "cotton wool" of daily "non-being," of habitual inattentiveness, to arrive at one, we must pass through the other, and we'll carry with us the content of that passing as we embark on our journey, though to stay in the state of arrival demands a concentrated experience of time to which our attentive skills can only be unequal. Yet in what way does Woolf's vaunted "we," multiply present throughout this material, express the connectedness that she surrenders to us?

Out of laboring to modify an abounding first-person plural, Woolf applies divided significations to the verb "to be," whose foremost sense (predicative, hinged on the prepositional phrase) she preserves until her penultimate clausal chain, when manifesting a condition metamorphoses into "being," into the fullness of coinciding-in-identity-with. After fixing on our angularity, connected with, parts of something more extensive than ourselves, we achieve agreement with the implemental character which defines us. But, because we begin in indirection, at a tangent to an entity more voluminous than ourselves, our names won't unfold us: there can be "no Shakespeare," "no Beethoven," "no God," no crowning maker, since the "whole world" overshadows the conceit of discreteness summoned by a lexical fiction to which the thing so named can't quite conform. Our coincidence must be with the mission of "the words," of "the music," "the thing itself" an instrumentality developed at divergent speeds through numberless millennia, a linchpin by whose service the wheel of the human world goes on spinning, seeing that any self, for Woolf, is backed by "ancestresses" and the specific circumstances they knew so long ago, ones supporting, sometimes breaking into, this present life. Of the things Woolf gives us here, one is beyond reference to, or undefined by, its use: the "whole" of "the work of art," in absolute congruence with itself. Yet the vision of such congruence, issuing from "shock['s]" concentrated force, will, by definition, fade. Its perceiver returns to the "cotton" blur, invoked by a name, unsure of her utility in a world she can't fully see, its curves revolving with and without her, all composing the background into which sudden sightedness breaks. However dim or broken, remembered "shock" nicks hollows in the uniformity of that blur, revives the experience of a whole superinduced by the near-artisanal tools that we are.

But what drives the telling of "the truth about this vast mass that we call the world"? How can we identify the teller?

Once detailing the "intuition" of her "philosophy," Woolf herself, the woman who studied Greek with Dr. George Warr, Clara Pater, and Janet Case—as Hermione Lee reminds us in the biography—alleges how "it is so instinctive that it seems given" to her, 'not made" by her, and we can mine the Platonic dialogue for a paradigm of such givenness. As early as the *Ion*, for example, Plato supplies us with a Socrates who quarries from his interlocutor whether the "art of poetry," of making, is rightfully a "skill" or the motion of a "divine power." Like all "rhapsodes," like all Homerian declaimers, Ion may be grouped with the "interpreters of interpreters," yet in what does poetic and declamatory expertise consist? If we intend to say, along with Plato's Socrates, that a "poet . . . cannot compose before he gets inspiration and loses control of his senses," so that "his reason has deserted him"; that "it is the god himself who speaks," addressing us "through" the mediate category of poets, themselves "nothing but the gods' interpreters, each possessed by his own possessing god," the skein of our logic will depend on our understanding of what interpretation imposes upon its practitioners, among whom Ion must be counted, as he listens to the exigencies in Homer's words while declaiming them.

In a note to his translation, Trevor John Saunders aids us in considering the reeling incumbent on the divine "mouthpiece": "only in Plato is the poet as passive" as such a representation avows; "on the ordinary Greek view," neither "the god" nor the poet is a "ventriloquist," since the former "consigns" his "message" or "information" to the poet "for casting" by him "into words, rhythms." Regardless of how the poet achieves that "casting," regardless of his knowing or being able to describe how he does it, "it is he himself who is the composer of his poetry, not the god." I want to twist all this together with the tonnage in Woolf's employment of "given," as the latter and what is done with it, made out of it, needn't be accounted exclusionary acts. While "possessed" by the "god," by the "whole" of the Woolfian "world," the "possessed" and her possessor stand yoked to each other by the explaining, in common, which interpretation enjoins on them. And, minding the "given" message, Woolf must dower it with the form through which the communicated becomes the communicable, an undertaking not unsuited to "reason." But in what ways might our conception of knowledge contribute to that dowering?

In the *Meno*, as he attempts to ascertain if "virtue" is "something that can be taught," Socrates argues that he can't "know a property of something" when he doesn't even know what that something "is." Consequently, the difficulty of knowledge inaugurates the dialogue's toils: "how on earth" are we "going to set up something" we don't know "as the object" of our "search"? Plato's actors and their readers seem enclosed in a question whose globularity disowns any conceptual action outside it; and, precisely due to that imprisonment, Socrates deems the question's undeclared argument a poor one. Explaining "how it fails," he moves to an outside epitomized by "the truths of religion," of which many "divinely inspired" poets speak. Those "truths" begin by presuming that the human "soul" is "immortal," locked in a cyclical pattern of apparent terminations and begettings, coming "to an end" merely to be "born again," without "extermination." "Born many times," never ending, "the soul" has "seen all things both here and in the other world, has learned everything that is." So, "when a man" recalls "a single piece of knowledge"—or when he learns it, bemused by how "ordinary language" mistakes recollection for learning—"there is no reason why he should not" discover "all the rest, if he keeps a stout heart and does not grow weary of the search," for "seeking and learning are in fact nothing but recollection." Yet, since religiosity postulates a whole in which each part inheres out of reverent obligation, must we find that the Platonic Socrates has substituted one circularity for another?

I include Woolf within the umbra cast by this question, as she and Plato appear to describe replacements at once familial and relentless: that of knowledge with "recollection," of experience with encountering "instincts already acquired by" repetitive "ancestresses" doomed to imparting identical lessons. We will be empowered to espy repetition in both cases only if we expunge all notion of the procedural necessary to "recollection" and to wrestling with the always "instinctive." For surely these actions, being actions, occur in time and under conditions that diverge from their sequentially foregoing and primordial origins; surely, we, Woolf, and Plato resemble the "boy" seeking geometrical "truths," "in company with" this particular Socrates whom he can't have known before the moment of interrogative "teaching." How we bring ourselves to that time, to those conditions, to that company, shapes what we make of recollected knowledge and articulates our experiential liberty, an instance of which is "A Sketch of the Past" itself, written on the cusp of world battle, among patterned "shocks" which Plato assists us in thinking out.

So far, the Platonic precedents for Woolf's "philosophy" advise us that poet and potential knower proceed in conjunction with a power, with a "soul," consecrated to disabusing us of the myth that any self writes, knows, or stands marooned in isolation. To appeal to virtue, to stand upright in its provident goodness, is thus to dedicate ourselves to remembering the associates among whom we live, presences which religious "truths" and Woolf's populous "we" both presuppose, even when we can't verify their palpability. But, in the *Philebus*, we learn that virtue begins as a problem, apart from its receptivity to being taught. Plato's Protarchus, "poised to take over" a "thesis" from "Philebus" that "the good is enjoyment, pleasure, delight and whatever is compatible with them," must contend with a Socrates who challenges that these "are not the good, but that reason, intellect, memory—not to mention their cognates, correct belief and true calculation—are far better than pleasure for all creatures capable of attaining them." The character of the highest excellence, unsettled at the dialogue's inception, is rendered more indeterminate by the "diversity within" the "good[s]" that wrangle for right definition, by the wobble between unity and plurality in "every single utterance," which "speech" appears to steady when it "identifies" the two in the process of our treating with words. It may be a part of Plato's project to show us how his foremost player disturbs the equipoise of Protarchus and his readers by divulging the "feature of human speech" which equates an identity-constructing "is" with the predication coincident with "far better than"; it may be that our stir towards the locality of "the good," whatever its determination, entangles us in the condensed difficulty which poise demands of those who profess to demonstrate its achievement. Yet, if qualities enlist their qualifiers, it is in the discussion of the "nature of memory," of "physical feeling," that we find Woolf's prototype for the "shock" which heralds any accession to "being."

And that discussion, as in the *Meno*, fails to question the existence of the "soul" already hypothecated—pledged to, adopted as self-evident—before the interplay by which dialectic is defined. But the dereliction of inquiry here belongs to how Plato's interlocutors foresee the body itself: if "the life of pleasure . . . is the good, it must lack nothing at all," so that if we "had pleasure," we'd have all we needed, a totality nevertheless obstructing our admission to the "reason, intellect, memory," without which we couldn't recognize our "feeling" of possessing the unimpeachable, an "all" condemning us not to "the life of a human being, but of a jellyfish or some sea creature," merely "a body endowed with life, a companion of oysters" shut up in a commotion of the sensorial, pseudonymous because barred from the cognition that harbingers what soul dispenses to its enfleshed instantiation. These ideas mean that a body is falsely named when seen denuded of the psyche whose radiation authorizes its alliance with the human. So bared, the body can never be enough; it becomes a lack, a negation, incapable of judging the "management" of the "life" ceded to it. Yet, if Socratic teaching shows Protarchus the possibility of differentiating between equivalence and predication, discloses that "two terms" anticipate "two things . . . not one," that "the good is not the same as the pleasant," this teaching must also combat the human desire to confound them.

Against confounding, the Platonic Socrates assembles "an immaterial system for the management of animate matter," since, with soul as the arbiter of body, the latter's conduct can be assessed, retrained by the adjudicator of incarnate comportment, a re-education revealing that the unseen both motorizes the body's visibility and administers its gestural repertory. Such two-ness confers on Protarchus, on his readers, a vocabulary for critiquing the specious sorcery of human pining—the enchantment that the world must requite us with what we ask of it, the two nouns, self and world, forever in antiphony—and leads to a "shock" intimate with the "nature of sensation," together with what can be realized from it.

Hypothesizing "about any physical feeling," speculating that "some are extinguished in the body before they penetrate to the soul," while "others penetrate both and create a sort of shock . . . peculiar to each part" yet "common to both," Socrates extends his bifurcating vision. Body differs from soul as the perturbation of one must deviate from that of the other, the soul's altitude over body in terms of value preparing the differential nature of the "shock" which psyche and soma share, traceable to the selfsame source. We may call this being "moved together," this "single experience" which pierces doubly, "sensation," with "memory" the name for its preservation, though the concept of rank returns when Plato gives us a Socrates who considers "recollection" as "what the soul does internally, without the body, when it resuscitates, as thoroughly as possible, the experiences it once shared" with the corporeal.

But these words underscore how the body drops away, already vaporous, always lost, under the principle that it should be animated by an energy other than itself. To lose the body is to empty the corporeal of all desire, to deny that desire is physical. While the aptitude for memory depends on the simultaneous piercing of skin and soul, provides the impulse towards "objects of desire," the argument here "is declaring that all drive, desire," and "authority, in every living creature, belongs to the soul": a proprietary license whose totalizing vigor ought to be matched by our avidity for disputing it.

Understood as lack, desire is founded on the longing for "replenishment," which only the faculty of memory can comprehend. But if "every living creature" strives "for the opposite to his present state"; if a "tendency towards the opposite . . . demonstrates that there is memory of the various opposites" to "various current states," jogs the "recollection" of an internal "soul," such internality is conditioned by the severance of outside from in, of flesh from psyche, and should cue our wonder at its nullifying industry. So negated with respect to praise, to any possible commendation, the body must be dangerous, its management a hazard. Before the spectre of that danger, uncoupled from the concept of worth due to the soul's radiating nimbus, all bodies become penurious things, strangely akin to those chunks of matter, inanimate, dead to valuation, which can't contest an authority disposed by necessity to manipulate them. The penury at the heart of these ideas, with regard to material things, forms much of what Woolf's world and our own have taken from antiquity, notwithstanding the glory of materiality sold to us so busily, for instance, by our contemporary advertising and fitness cultures—and by Trump's much photographed "lifestyle" itself. Yet the abounding poverty at work in the *Philebus* needs to be read in more than one way. We must look at whom the "denial" of desiring corporeality seeks to aim.

When Protarchus and Philebus declare that pleasure is equal to "the good," they attribute goodness to all pleasures, classifying pleasure as the "most similar thing of all to pleasure, as being itself in relation to itself." Assimilating relation to identity, plurality to oneness, they reveal the body as a magnified thing, an "itself," an organ for the reception of pleasures, identical because one can always be substituted for any other. The "thesis" of equivalence, since it entails the interchangeability of all desires conducing to "the good," thus holds to a disinterest in, an incapacity for, judgment, discrimination, complexity, terms which pinpoint that one idea can't be made to fit the world. Such are the characters of his colleagues that Socrates must dissolve the thickening redundancies they keep to, such the exertions that Plato tests our capability of seeing. Even so, if we assent to Wittgenstein's disclosure, in *The Blue Book*, that "philosophy, as we use the word, is a fight against the fascination which forms of expression exert upon us," we should hesitate in order to ask: has Socrates subdued one fascination by deputizing another in its place; does his maker propose that we concur with this supplanting of the body by what the body is not?

But to answer the second question in the affirmative is to believe that the maker must be the equivalent of what he makes, to barter one name for another, a belief which nearly every Platonic dialogue controverts. Its method of argumentation neither apodeictic— concerned with demonstrating proof—nor self-explanatory, the dialogue, because it seldom shows us outright the intent goading on its progress, incites in readers the very inferentiality by which it's come to be there, on the page. And, since it represents the conditions from which the groundwork of a detailed human conversation can be derived, that page originates from a hand whose activities must be accounted for, not from the *ex nihilo* subsequent to the conflation of "two things" into one. Obliged to inspect those conditions, to bring them in under the circumspection of our eyes, we may begin to approach their founder, though his creations impart to us that he's always elsewhere.

Readers can venture to see in the depth afforded by the twofold distances between eye and page, between eye and the designer of that page, a Socrates who diminishes the density of the body so as to carry his colleagues to the "threshold" of "the good" from which they can survey desire, once blind because it could have no truck with analysis, misconstruing satiety as the sole criterion of evaluation. Facing his associates' closed-circuit of body, desire, good, Socrates must admit that circuit as his conversational starting place and undo it, if he's to advocate for an outside in which this wiring together submits to critical estimation. He disperses the heft of the body, fictionalizing it, etherealizing it, neutralizing its efficacy, the strain to dematerialize the body decreeing the devastations waiting to be wrought by those who, imagining "the good" as "the most perfect thing of all," might "track it down and aim for it, with no concern for anything" not "ultimately accompanied by goodness." So thinned of purport, the body is stripped of its capacity to engender the inventory of actions by which it would consume the world, dissolving "goodness" in "itself."

Of course, such dispersal saves both that world's constituents and our Socratic comrades, their apparent weightlessness readying them "to love the truth and to go to any lengths for its sake." Unmade with respect to what they thought they knew, they find all the substantiality of the body—the belief in its power to grasp, to control, to guide—transferred to the soul, which "resembles a book." And, "when memory coincides with perception," psychic faculties seem "to write words . . . in the soul," their "truth" resulting from that coincidence. Yet when memory and perception, no longer coinciding, are "mistaken in their object," "an artist" in "the soul's work-force" forms "internal images" of a concordance whose falseness can be settled by the soul's facility for adjudication. "True" or "false" in its "contact" with the world, the soul becomes a "picture" of the following paradox: an immateriality capable of "making . . . correct assessment," according to "law and order" always administered by a "truth," by a cause, completely "different" from what depends on it "for generation." Such diction describes a rightness forever beyond what we proclaim of it, its religiosity a universalizing force distinguishing between itself and the inclination of all bodies regarding it, concepts which Protarchus and Philebus couldn't have reached, had they tarried at believing in the unthinking body, recognizable only through the measureless character of its longings.

But I remember, in the *Parmenides*, for instance, that Plato supplies us with a Socrates who can't remove himself from the quandary intrinsic to "abstract ideas" and "the things which partake of them." Questioned "if there is an idea" of "hair, mud, dirt"—or "anything else particularly vile and worthless"—distinct "from the things with which we have to do, or not," Socrates can simply intone a "no": they "are such as they appear to us," for "it would be quite absurd to believe that there is an idea of them; and yet I am sometimes disturbed by the thought that perhaps what is true of one thing is true of all." Even for the Socrates who teaches others that entities differ from the forms of expression we level at them, the problem, the intervallic space, stretched between desire and its objects remains.

That remaining parades how the problem is ours. We're born to it, inheritors of the distances in which all things coexist and whose extent, despite our being "disturbed" by it, promises our propensity to think, to see, to move, to make something out of how we participate in action. They become, those disturbances, those "shock[s]," the distance we live by, the range of sight allowing for the connectedness that we can, or can't, conceive of valuing. Think how the nation's climate would shift, if Trump and those who follow him found it possible to question how they see. The old examples are there. They can be listened to. And the listening ought to form a part of our responsible human labor.

The Life in the Sky Comes Down Essays, Stories, Essay/Stories

Eighteen

The wolf is entitled to the lamb.
The Mountain Wreath (1847)

Hearken unto me, fellow creatures. I who have dwelt in a form unmatched with my desire, I whose flesh has become an assemblage of incongruous anatomical parts, I who achieve the similitude of a natural body only through an unnatural process, I offer you this warning: the Nature you bedevil me with is a lie. Do not trust it to protect you from what I represent, for it is a fabrication that cloaks the groundlessness of the privilege you seek to maintain for yourself at my expense. You are as constructed as me; the same anarchic Womb has birthed us both. I call upon you to investigate your nature as I have been compelled to confront mine. I challenge you to risk abjection and flourish as well as have I. Heed my words, and you may discover the seams and sutures in yourself.
Susan Stryker (1994)

The Life in the Sky Comes Down Essays, Stories, Essay/Stories

Figuring Images (5): Listening to the Dead

For months now, I've seemed to live in a crowd of stories. I've got a lot of company there.

The second epigraph to Edna O'Brien's recent novel, *The Little Red Chairs*, takes me close to the looming character of these stories, how *The Mountain Wreath* argues, long before the Yugoslav Wars that burned through the 1990s, that the wolf and the lamb can be joined together by the human claim to entitlement, so that both become our surrogates. The human-wolf enacts what the strong do, propelled by natural law, while the human-lamb succumbs to a victimhood ordained at birth. These enchained performances, looped into a whole by the qualifying vision at which our species excels, even when misaligned, by the effort to conceive of rightfulness, justice, and their costs, will be significant for Nietzsche when he maintains, in 1887, that "the large birds of prey," tangling "little lambs" between their beaks, show what strength exacts from the beings who must be identical with its exactions. Hearing such tales that appear to represent the family of human and non-human animals, both groups blurred by a metaphorical athletics, I pause.

I'm thinking of bodies deemed actionable by the law that purports to order what can and can't be done to them, of a cluster of southern states busily identifying those Americans who should be debarred from entering particular bathrooms, clarifying that persons who love the wrong bodies, who inhabit the wrong bodies due to a gender fluidity unworthy of the time that it takes to read them, ought to be rendered vulnerable to living outside legal protection, since they abide, anyway, in an elsewhere so distant from those who judge them. I think of bodies that cross the wrong borders to remake what *home* might mean, bodies fleeing from the bones and blood and dust behind them, only to meet, at best, a partial welcome. I hear Donald Trump and Ted Cruz, along with their colleague-rivals who targeted the White House as their aim, mistake the shout for what speech can do. And I listen to the dead, to Virginia Woolf, to Plato, as they tell a different story through the millennia dividing them about bodies, about what readers owe to the struggle to think of them.

Before turning to how Woolf adapts the antecedent of Plato's "shock," so important to the *Philebus*, I search for what textual forerunners bequeathed to the woman who read them, for what they offer to those who follow her. I recall Plato's Socrates and his transcendent noun phrase, whether in the *Philebus* or the *Republic*, where "justice" shadows forth "the good," and find that this coming forth shows Socrates asserting, for his interlocutors, that the latter unendingly embraces the former. All we may be said to have here below are reflections of "the good," refractions of its breadth and depth, yet that statement must be qualified by Plato's Socratic visions regarding our flawed humanity, from which Socrates himself can't be excepted. If readers attend to that qualification, we come to how inductive processes concerning the concept of "the good" occur always in relation to those towards whom such processes are steered, so that we never achieve a philosophic discourse, or any discourse at all, outside the grounding of an audience and its frailties, its conditions, never gain the footing by which we could hope to scan a hoard of precepts underivable, unadulterated, absolute. If this is true, we populate an aporia, an undecidability, which nevertheless may be useful for us, its readers. Because we can't know, finally, what the Platonic Socrates thinks concerning "the good," for that thinking, as evidenced by the page, stands in relation with other speakers, "the good," notwithstanding its admissible status as myth, narrative, image, or truth, escapes its incarnations. There will be, everlastingly, a beyond to the circumstances in which we feel ourselves engrossed, even if we can't stop there, embosomed in its clasp.

The Socrates whom Plato ventilates for us respects how the transcendent concept as such must be elsewhere, in excess of our pronouncements on the subject of it, remote from the mastership of human appetites, regardless of its being myth or narrative or undertaken to accommodate to what a specific audience can just tolerate hearing—or of its potential truth-value. But, while we never inhabit "the good" itself in Platonic thinking, we can sample proximity to its avatars. Among these we should tally "correct assessment," though that proximal relation will be burdensome enough for us to heed, considering the human desire to think equationally by means of operations tussling for a simplistic comprehension of unity. Here, I look back to the *Parmenides*, for if "it would be . . . absurd" to think that the things we fail to devote ourselves to participate in notions of value, the absurdity is solely ours: we'll have raised so high, as if miming the seeming guidance of Plato's characters, "abstract ideas" assorting their terrestrial "images"; we'll have submerged "hair, mud, dirt" in the element appropriate to them, in the ground that must be "dirt" and that prevails, merely to suffer our sovereignty over it. Conceptual union and its absence become our bestowments, produced by a falsifying vision. They repeat us. And this is one lesson that Trump enacts, daily.

Yet, even according to these texts' apparent terms, we can't say with certainty that Plato's Socrates occupies or is habituated to "the good," as that abstract noun continues comprehensively beyond the claiming of any selfhood. This fact remains its virtue and ours. Since we're unable to usurp it, to subjugate it, "the good" can only be inhospitable to those human activities which scheme to eat their object. In consequence, our Platonic materials advise us to reflect on, to think critically about, our desires, to position ourselves at a tangent to what they command of us, so that we might touch but not intersect with them. We need both to experience and to analyze our desiring in order to salvage ourselves from engulfment and to preserve the world from the annihilation that our hunger's appeasement would produce. Existing in relation to them, that hunger is not the world and not "the good."

The incessant freedom from arrest, whether or not we're intended to assent to "the good" as myth, accommodation, or verity, divulges the vigilant sophistication of Plato as a writing-mind and that mind's quadruple covenant with its readers. As his words call forth the prudent alertness essential to any study of a wisdom unrevealed by the surfaces of the said, coax our awareness that interpretive acts never take place in transparency, refocus the lights by which we read, so that the *how* of comprehension can neither be ready-made nor unconditioned, fashion form and content as reciprocal envoys—Plato, uncaptured, unimprisoned, unrepresented by the verbal shapes he gives us, cautions against our bewitchment by, our fascination with, messages foretokening our partnership in their reception and transference, since those messages won't decipher themselves. To entreat our participation in composing the contours of any message is to brake the latter's implementation in the world, to portion out a lull soliciting our responsibility in the fight not to beguile others with an expression by which no person should be arrested. And, if Plato himself can bolt from the texts he circulates among us, that expertise in breaking free from detention calls on us to answer it, to remember that we must bridle up at seeing any text as a stopgap for charged contemplation or as a stopover in which, idling, we might doze.

Their forger's refusal to be confined, rejoined by our dexterity in remarking how faraway he is from us, motions towards our discovery that Platonic texts develop from—and prompt the readerly acceptance of—those remotenesses, those gulfs, those intervals, through which we perceive the perceptible and are perceived ourselves. Rather than condemning them to mutual banishment, the standing apart of writer and reader permits their connection, so long as we acknowledge distances as the means by which we commit ourselves to sight. Yes, the range of their intermediary spaces may fluctuate: in many texts, Plato mimes, by way of supposed direction and in dialogic form, speeches whose fictiveness lies in their being authorless, while others, recounting in the present a past whose totality won't be resuscitated, offer us speakers interposed between ourselves and the urgencies they set about reviving. Nevertheless, even in fluctuation, distanced sight endures, a lens for the recognition that inclining near is not a given but a movement—earned.

This movement implied by any resistance to detainment, to imprisonment, appeals to Plato's readerly imperative. We must spurn, for example, equating ourselves as readers outside the *Republic* with the many-partnered Socrates inside it. Though we resemble that preeminent voice and its fellows to the extent that our desiring transactions, by necessity, outreach our needs and their object, mistaken for a terminal satisfaction somehow never to be forfeited, once we become the equivalents of Plato's characters, we extinguish the text, along with our aptitude for interpreting it. Yet we can countervail such imposture by creating, by clearing, by opening up, a critical discontinuity between ourselves and what we read in order to decide how, as Socrates and his comrades watch a *polis* "coming into existence" in speech, the one noble lie, the "magnificent myth that would . . . carry conviction" to the city, is a residuum of conceptual activities closely aligned with the hazards basic to unconscious metaphoric usage. I mean: if it's the commerce of metaphors to over-naturalize their own behaviors, to betray equivalence as already accomplished, rather than as our manufacture, that commerce serves the human need to aver the wholeness of the world, without recognizing that proposed wholeness may demonstrate the fiat of a maker's desire for it, which, in the doing, erases how (so often) many of us proceed uncritically before integrities which we ourselves fashion.

The nobility here, the magnificence, evolves from the power of the myth to honor the mortal fragilities that it speaks to. And our examination of the mythic, our regarding the circumstances that give birth to it, together with how its claim to "increase . . . loyalty" may incite consent, makes it conceivable for readers outside the text to see the integral as a speculation masking itself as fact, a camouflaging we might guard against, if we were to reflect on our own need to confuse a making-method with the world. That world, or another noun in its place, capable of transcending the figurations that we sling at it, remains richly other than what we do within its precincts. It won't be, in any final sense, confounded. "Amorous," erotic, we may construe ourselves as the kin of Glaucon; in our eroticism, inflamed, we may love the part to the exclusion of the "whole," as though love were a fire whose burning object could only be itself, intensified. Whether or not we distinguish between ourselves and his Socratic audience, the inventor of the *Republic* reminds us, by his very absence, that we don't live bound inside the pages of a book, that not living there permits us to picture, to visualize, to entertain, the "story" both spun on and fixed to the fibers of the page. Not living there fosters our awareness that the *eros* piloting our fictions, our telling of tales, can't be the ground but is made from our comportment in relation to the ground itself.

Preserving these distinctions, we find that the "story" fails due to the instabilities of its narration. But instabilities, because his characters seem unable to identify them, are among Plato's gifts to us: loitering over them, naming them, we accept their fathering in another place and confess our obligation to judge the worthiness of our own paternity. And what does Socrates, the maker of stories, contrive in the presence of a Glaucon, whose amorousness longs to light upon itself in the things it loves? He images a creation-myth which naturalizes "loyalty" to the dialogic city, even as its manner of recounting dishonors the interdictions at play in the upbringing, the education, of those "Rulers and Soldiers" bred to administer governance. Yet their schooling, the Socratic myth insists, "happened to them only in a dream," a visual tale different from the actual world, occurring within that world, but other than it. Accordingly, if "we begin by telling children stories" because childhood "is the time when they are easily moulded," when "any impression we choose to make leaves a permanent mark"; if we "must start to educate" the psyche "before training the body"—all the strictures of that tutelage subsist in the relation of a simile, a likeness, bending towards the "reality" glinting below. In order to arrive at foundational turf, the following restrictions, once approved, must be penetrated. Prospective "Guardians," for "fear of catching the infection in real life," must refrain from "acting" a "disgraceful part on the stage" in view of how mimesis, when prolonged into adulthood, establishes habits which "become second nature." To inoculate all against the virus of imitation, "if the poet never concealed his own personality," his poetic narrative, "devoid of representation," would liberate any audience from mimetic blight. To misrepresent "the nature of gods and heroes" is to commit "the worst fault possible"; because anything "not harmful" can't "do harm," the "god" really "is good" and "must be so described," regardless of generic concerns. Without "deceit or falsehood in action or word," the godly "does not change himself, nor deceive others, awake or dreaming, with visions or words or special signs."

To sum up this "dream," soon to be absorbed into the familial essence of citizenship: we begin in plasticity, are perfectly educable and can be perfected from without, as if bodily behaviors simply reproduced those teachings which the soul had suckled from. In contrast to human flux, the "god" must be "good"; he doesn't lie, doesn't change, so that divinity, idealized, is in analogy with the Ideas, against whose permanence all phenomena occur. Natal oscillations may unite humankind here, though the subsequent myth attempts to cancel them out. Regarded "as brothers," the city's residents are indistinguishable from the earth that mothers them.

Or so the Socratic progenitor of myth would persuade "our whole community" to believe.

Neither poets nor wholly admitting that they engage in talking/writing stories, Plato's characters see themselves as founders of a state, whose gradual "word-picture," however phantasmagoric, might help them to remember the necessity of pursuing "justice with wisdom" in an already founded world. As authors of an "ideal" civic structure, they should know the type of story that "the poets must produce" and, rejecting any that don't conform to that model, need not write tales themselves. But, fascinated by the gleam of igniting, among its citizens, fealty to "the state and to each other," Socrates can't quit the seduction of conjuring stories. He won't have the impulse to bewitch idealized out of him, even if a prior education legislated, in a "dream," that the imitator may be surpassed by his imitations, so long as such surpassing holds to the stricture against change, against flux, something that Socrates and his figurative profligacy risk, on the page.

Yet we who read him, who keep watch over the invisible hand behind his words, ought to note how the inaugural myth is as doused in figuration as the pedagogy preceding it, observe how both conflate custom and nature, *nomos* and *physis*, in order to divine the stability designed to render them connectable. Though education and myth seem in opposition, together they struggle to stay human lability by means of ordaining its representations, the former taking mimetic virulence as an almost organic given, the latter enrolling a communal brotherhood in which the "god" has added metal to the composition of every member—gold to the "Rulers," silver to the "Auxiliaries," iron and bronze to the "farmers and other workers," so that the metallurgical figure will assign each his "proper value" in the place where he belongs. But all this metaphorical labor describes a materiality prophesying ruin when the state has "Guardians" outside the rule of gold.

Underlying both tales is, of course, the fear of human vulnerability to change and evanescence, a certain worry in Trump's wrangling for and achievement of the presidency. Before that fear, all of us (any "I") are so easily the victims of our figures, so easily jeopardize the *polis* that professes to order us. While the conflation of *nomos* and *physis* unavoidably domesticates religion, understands religion as subsumed under culture's shadow, if we deem such fabricated perspicuity a regulative fiction, we might vary the pattern that we make of it, since, like the real in relation to it, our fiction is never unalloyed, static, fixed. The failure of any metaphor to stabilize its objects is akin to inexhaustibility, a paragon of success due to that failure's steadfastness, advancing what won't be exhausted as a value in which we inhere, because it supports us.

Everything I discuss here presumes a distinction between Plato-the-maker and the image of Socrates in our texts. The latter themselves, born of a wakefulness to the fact of human fallibility and desire, stage readers' appetitive maneuverings as the breeding ground for the metaphors by which we construe what it means to live. Yet, if the customary linguistic deportment of metaphor matches two entities via the figurative representation of equivalence, it needn't follow that we should discern the figure itself as a mere substitution for what it appears, with facility, to coagulate. Instead, we can grasp that the figure, when understood analytically by its maker and by those to whom it's addressed, prizes the corporeality which is, after all, its index. As the figure represents how the twinned materialities of perceiver and perceived adhere to each other, it endures being always double in at least this sense: it describes a making-method in contact with something outside it, and its description carries the weight of that transport. For these reasons, metaphors don't replace the real with a fiction; they attest to the real being there, to the complex nature of the real itself. Regarding possible Socratic fascination with the figurative: all bewitchments aren't equal; some allow us to see more rather than less, such as those metaphoric couplings through which we who read Plato's Socrates can realize that sightedness is never incontestable, that it must be borne witness to by our deliberations over it.

The attestations I trace out seem potentially ethical acts to me, a seeing through our skills at beguilement. The obligation—incessant, magisterial—for each of us to grant, and to give testimony to, those interdependencies whereby the real is composed directs me to Maurice Merleau-Ponty's ideas in his posthumously published *The Visible and the Invisible*. There, we find illuminated an "intercorporeity" in which the little private world of each thing isn't juxtaposed to that of all the others but surrounded by it, levied off from it, and all together are an "intercorporeal being," the surface of a depth, which, "inexhaustible," we can properly term the visible. And our always multiplying species will never be its owners. If we can't lay claim to the titular ownership of this intercorporeality because we belong to it, because we survive and perish by virtue of it, each thing is bound up, opens on, is endlessly interrelated, with other things, so that the world becomes a web of the relational; so that no thing abides in isolation from other things; so that isolation, like unhampered congress, numbers among our fictions, reprehensible, unavailing, if not wakened to.

While systems thinking champions such ideas, as treated by Ludwig von Bertalanffy in *General Systems Theory*, by Bela H. Banathy in *Designing Social Systems in a Changing World*, in *The Guided Evolution of Society*, and while much of quantum theory reinforces them, I don't ask the sciences to stand surety for the power or for the truth-functions of those ideas. Rather, I propose that, from them, we might envision an ethics of the "intercorporeal," which would argue for the virtues in comprehending that we never stand alone, fall alone, live, die alone. We *are* with respect to the intertwinements of which phenomena are made. To believe otherwise is to beguile others in a darkness of our own fabrication, in an obscurity without use, to counter that we must by necessity be mistaken in our objects, even though they aren't quite ours, since we'll have breathed among them.

Having scanned some of Woolf's Platonic ancestry, I contemplate how the woman who studied Greek with Clara Pater, with Janet Case, as Hermione Lee's biography details, modulates a "shock" whose textual inception seems to underscore the division between "being" and "non-being," so key to any reading of Woolf's "A Sketch of the Past." I begin my contemplation, however, by approaching the organism which Plato and Woolf regard according to dissimilar assumptions, to variant ends. I start with the body that "walks, eats, sees things, deals with what has to be done," with what can't be dodged, with the faculty of judgment urgently considered by both thinkers. For these minds, telling "the truth about this vast mass that we call the world" implies an account of the soma whose dispositions affect the revolving of that world, given our great numbers. But, below any recital of physicality, underneath our two writers' discrepant viewpoints concerning its valuation, we encounter this: the body and its sensorium *stop*. Our experience of the corporeal is limited by its termination, a limiting whose attributes we can neither review nor report on, as the ordeal of that curb undoes us. Even our capacity for asserting that *the ordeal undoes us* exemplifies the manner in which our very language supposes that self and body are separable, that the former must survive, or disengage from, the concretion which hauls it along the curvature of the world, so far as syntactic logic admits the announcement that I will outlast my undoing. The soma's disgrace rests on its being doomed to desert us, speakers who negotiate grammars trumpeting a continuance that any grammar can't, in fact, deliver.

Yet the foundering of that delivery, while it summarizes the body's danger, its exposure to a decline which we may not know how to countenance, abets our endeavors to compensate for it. Perhaps from desertion, from declination, issue those displacements which, in their prevalence, Plato desires we should own to. Disbanded from the body, mind, self, and soul become synonymous and eternal, their everlastingness a reparation for fleshly defeat. Nevertheless, the eternity promulgated here, once elevated as a measure of excellence, is as though upraised over the things of the world, over "hair, mud, dirt" and their non-human analogues, all deemed equal to "how they appear to us," to the inertness we read in them, as Plato's Socrates insists in the *Parmenides*. We who aren't their kinsmen, according to this stance, and whose concept of perpetuity originates in the need to disconnect from a soma which decays, without end.

Woolf may inherit these ideas. As one of his many heirs, she may accept that Platonic indirection starts with the accidental from which ascends, over the range of the dialogues, the purposing, the planning, the schematizing, which Socrates and his companions uplift by way of exhibiting how flux can be transformed into the invariant. But the method itself disappoints, uproots, any reader's longing to halt at fascination with the invariable. In view of how the circumstantial initiates the dialogues' sequenced thinking, given a different set of circumstances, another assortment of persons and their inclinations, everything would be otherwise. Consequently, though our Platonic texts appear to affiliate externality with "non-being," to federate the internal, the incorporeal, with a "being" always beyond decrepitude, their structures surrender us to the extrinsic as our foundation and as our founding trouble. Woolf extends that trouble, that ambiguity lengthened between the touched and the touching, to what Merleau-Ponty espouses as "les choses," the things we contact and are contacted by. Through such extension, Woolf prepares us for a transcendence that integrates human physicality and the things among which it lives, notwithstanding her claims to the contrary.

When she studies her habit, at "six or seven," of looking at her face in the glass, reveals that "the looking-glass shame" has lasted all her life, that its duration uncovers how her "natural love for beauty was checked by some ancestral dread," Woolf concedes that such shame failed to interfere with her feeling "ecstasies and raptures," provided that both were disconnected from her own body. Yet, rather than registering a discrete fact, being ashamed or afraid of the body is to despair at learning that the flesh can't be seen by itself, solitary, anomalous, whole, just as yearning to unhitch our regarding the body from the means by which we scrutinize it, or to sever feeling from carnality, is to confirm insufficiency as our heritage. Unlike Woolf herself, I fit our "ancestral" lack of insularity to the image that she sketches a page later: if she was "looking in the glass one day when something in the background moved," that movement, that aliveness, pertains to spatiality, to bodies, and to the mirror that donates them a piecemeal representation. Certainly, "the glass" can't fasten to itself the things hedged in by the rigidity of its frame, since the traffic of the body, of our desiring beauty, of space, of things themselves, overtops all representational circumscriptions. I coordinate this spilling over with Merleau-Ponty's admission that we're "never at the thing itself." The experience of disconnection from the body bespeaks the entitlement of having once been anchored there, insulated from the overspill bequeathed to flesh and to things, though both can neither be perceived nor arrived at as if they were lone, one, entire.

Even the mirror thwarts the myth of insulation when we move away from it. And that thwarting lies like a ground underneath the Woolfian "ecstasies and raptures" that "A Sketch of the Past" takes such care to picture. Since her narrations of ecstatic and rapturous incidents end with feeling how "it is almost impossible" that the self should be here, with an inability to describe being seized by a time and place which drum up a vibrative hum along the frets of the senses, Woolf's first person usage airs that any "I" is never at the thing itself, never knows parity with the irresolvable by which selfhood may be characterized or with the certitude of being altogether taken. What holds true for persons presides, in this instance, over things themselves, as the two divisions inhabit a mutual distancing. "I" am that which encroaches on things, they are those entities that seem to encroach on "me," and both warrant the spaces between them to preserve the world they share.

But, while she succeeds to Plato's inaugural "shock," to a causality effacing bodily significance in order to elevate a soul fated to judge its relations with animate matter beyond the limit of a single life; while Platonic fiction struggles to save the matter of the world from the wreckage produced by our indiscriminate coveting, do Woolf's "sudden shocks" ask us to partition off the "real thing" from "appearances," to divide value from the body? The differential immensities of "being" and its apparent opposite needn't destine both to compartmentation. Rather, their differences secure the possibility of reciprocal encroachment. To express this idea in other terms, when adducing disconnection from the body as the criterion for "ecstasy" and "rapture," Woolf doesn't presume the nugatory status of the flesh. She cites fleshliness as a perplexity worth the neural expense of aspiring to survey it, to "explain it," an aspiration which accepts that neurological enterprises assume the material in which they're enmeshed. Though both narratives of the body (as pulled away from itself, as taken by an outside it can't thoroughly describe) suppose a physicality exalted or transfixed, the following assurance predetermines their reception: even as our alignment with the corporeal, with "appearances," with a thing identifiable as real, like any acquaintanceship with connectivity, can never be wholly prearranged, the indirectness of our pathways to alliance invokes our aptitude for edging towards its accomplishment, despite the latter's necessary momentariness. If we consent to considering, with Merleau-Ponty, that we ought to pass from the thing "as identity" to the thing "as difference," as transcendence, as behind, beyond, as always faraway, we resemble the things among which we live in compliance with the multidirectionality ascribable to the human, to the inanimate, both sustained by an "intermundane" space, which confers on their many variations a more than uniparous birth. Once acceding to these considerations, we join Woolf in being carnalities inclusive of, but not assimilable to, the properties of which we're made, so that possession by right or force becomes annulled (forever imperfect, unfinished), due to our prepositional grip on the body that any language allows us to call our own.

If memory and forgetting are discontinuous with regard to experience, our sense of self-foundership must be remade, reclaimed, as will Woolf's ability to "put the severed parts together" under the briefly unifying "blow." When she wonders, however, if "things we have felt with great intensity have an existence independent of our minds," Woolf imagines that, one day, she "shall fit a plug into a wall" and, listening to the past, discover garden and nursery emanating from a current by which "we shall be able to live our lives through from the start," as though to listen were to bypass the flexuosity, the bending in, central to interpretation. Yet this deposit of feeling and prospect shows us how a woman, leaning a present ear in the direction of garden and nursery (murmurous, distant, strangely close), would heed them not alone through the technology of a mediating "plug" but thanks to contemporary attention tilting towards, bordering on, those sounds lost to a past in need of decipherment because that past could never simply unspool itself. Such near sight-reading exertions, under the possible future of Woolf's image, signal the "third voice" that we hear again as she speaks to Leonard, her husband, as "Leonard speaks" to her, both sensing a tertiary thing circulating among the said, the sonority that they give rise to, together, made actual by acoustics, by time, by place, into which other sonorities may break. As Woolf sketches this past that doesn't seem to die, as we read her, so much intervenes: "light glows"; an "apple becomes a vivid green"; an owl throws its vowels under the window, each not an aid to disconnection but to our remembrance that what appears to come between, the "vessel afloat on sensation," the "plate exposed to invisible rays," a voice born of other voices, produces the relations of which words, music, and "the thing itself" are made, the latter a whole other than, though proposed by, the multiplicity of its parts.

To say that we don't live "confined" to the body, to the part, is to envision a kinship with "scenes" through which floods a "reality" greater than, yet allowing for, evident circumscription, to invite the "shock" whose violence tells us that the body's "sealing matter," by definition, cracks open on to other things. If our Platonic texts emerge from a top-down construction which situates, at its core, the body forever constrained by a soul it can't see, Woolf's "life-writing," her writing on behalf of life, trains itself on presences seen and unseen, their interdependence exceeding the limits of any sketch. We can remark, with her, that "I see myself as a fish in a stream; deflected; held in place; but cannot describe the stream," knowing how the Heraclitean simile approaches a fluidity whose dimensions we'll persistently fail to measure with adequate fullness, although they grant persons and things a kind of swimming, that the courage to admit the incapacity to describe, comprehensively, is itself a way to swim.

For my part, I belong to what Maggie Nelson's *The Argonauts* pictures in many ways, a body "non-heteronormative" because of how I dress it, bejewel it, what I do with it, with other male bodies that my own answers an impassioned *yes* to. Like many of my kind, I refuse to be thrown in a crowd outside the law and its vision of the right that it means to enforce—

or, under pressure, to reconceive. Like all members of my species, I'm neither wolf nor lamb. They aren't our ghosts, our masks; they've no business with the concepts that humans often misapply. To turn to the Heraclitus whose ideas were always there as a basis for Plato to work away from, so that he could hold up something against the time and change that would erode it, and with Woolf, I say: the stretch of rippling water that we swim in is our home. And no one should be pushed out of it. Or the swimming.

Nineteen

The Life in the Sky Comes Down Essays, Stories, Essay/Stories

What Betsy Was

Fin and Flesh

For years beyond counting, she lived far under water among the green things. Their shine resembled that light before the storm comes above ground, as if seen through the veins of a new leaf held close to the eye, in a time so distant that its tale must have been whispered in her ear by a voice she no longer recalled how to speak back to. She'd look, in daylight, at the angles of the rocks that jut up from the sand below, whose bottom she was afraid to find. She'd float over the sunken ferns, the stems many-leaved and waving, watch the fish nestling there whom she called her scaly sisters, their shared kin as much a mystery to her as her own name. She thought that the moon, when it came, rose from and hovered a little above the surface of the water. That surface was the sky she knew. She'd see her hair drift ahead of her, the color of a tongue after it's licked an apple for too long, though apples were things that she forgot, every day, except one. She forgot that she'd had a father who threw the noose of his love around her, that he condemned her to the sea because she could only refuse the rub of that noose against her skin. To fail at returning love was to be hurled into joining the heave, the burden, of water. She forgot that, once, her body didn't taper to a fin, greeny, glinting, its fan and flap suspending her in one spot, if she chose, without end. But each year, for a single day, she remembered every part of it.

A great wind below the water hefts her up, level with what she thinks of as the sky that had filled her eyes. Pushed higher, lifted on air, she sees the water lipped by a chalk cliff coast and foaming beneath a tufty place, translucent, always moving. Then, shoved down, down, she meets the beach with its shale and pebbles and mussels, their shells opening in the sudden light. She finds her fin given way to two conch-colored legs, longer than the ferns she loved. And standing, she starts to walk across the

ground that she'll come to know, briefly, and forget again.
She Looks at the Boy in the Courtyard

All this Betsy von Furstenberg must be thinking, paused on the other side of the John Drew Theatre's stage exit door, that East Hampton sky an iris, moodily blued by afternoon sun. Betsy imagines that the boy she turns to, whose name she believes is Bruce though it should be Bran, due to the grainy life of his curls, makes such a story of her while he sits, curled up on grass in the middle of the courtyard, waiting. He's one of the apprentices trained to bang at the rising up of sets, to work the lights, to run over lines with actors, their memory skills gone missing, like the sun that comes and goes, like this boy's name that wafts in and out, but out of what, she can't put an apt word to. He aims his eyes at her piled up hair, dyed tomato red for the part of Mrs. Prentice in Joe Orton's *What the Butler Saw*, the words lost to her a few moments ago on stage, so that Edward Albee sent her to refocus, outside. Betsy and the boy may perform in different ways for the man that she calls Edward, whom Bruce has been schooled to refer to as Mr. Albee, but both watch for the edging up of his left eyebrow, which would be partnered by thunder, if it could. It's 1972, years after *Who's Afraid of Virginia Woolf* became a stand-in for his name, and the summer repertory company that Edward directs will fill the theatre with Orton's frenzy for all of July. That ruckus begins tomorrow, opening night. Betsy still worries at the words, at their rhythms. She moves closer to the boy, the curtain of his hair loosed across his eyes. Before running lines and standing under a linden in the courtyard's center, its buds slowly unfolding, she scrolls in her head through the things she's heard of him.

He's on the far side of 14 and fevered by a man named Stephen, who's over thirty. They met at one of those late after rehearsal parties, in a house larger than a ship, by a wood-rimmed pool into which naked bodies plunged, like hasty dolphins. Stephen's promise to drive Bruce home ended at his Amagansett cottage, by the dunes. You could hear wind pulling on the beach plums and piping its long vowels through the apple tree, while Stephen arced the boy's neck back, kissing unshaved skin, and the stars seemed strung from every leaf. On the bed below Warhol's portrait of Stephen, paid for with his mother's money and which captured each black wave, finely gelled, Bruce misplaced what thinking was. He remembered it later, at home, when his father punched him up against the front door, and Bruce walked through the bits that were left of it. He rode his bike to the cottage, though Stephen lay in the dunes with an older boy, their sounds mingling among rolling water. Bruce broke a window, unlocked the door, and waited in bed for the Stephen who never came. And this is what love calls on us to do, Betsy thinks, shatter windows, splinter doors, and we answer it with a hunger that knows no end. Looking down at the boy while he stares up at her, Betsy sees shard-like things, dropped in the middle of his eyes. Their sound would make a shudder of the air, she knows, if he were to merge with the power to pull them out.

Staging Motion

Betsy flails her arms, as Mr. Albee insists, but really she's wondering about the horizontal people. They're those who know themselves by the speed with which they can hurry across a stage, across grass, across anything flat enough to hold them up. Betsy's described them to Bruce, who should be Bran, in grand contrast to the vertical ones, capable of staying in a single place and looking out. At this dress rehearsal, she doesn't know what belonging to that tribe would mean.

Was it the right decision, Betsy asks herself, to play at living in other people's skins or to sport at raising up the Mrs. Prentice whom Orton races in a sprint, page after page, hustling for more love, more love, before Kenneth Halliwell pounded the body that wrote her into pieces, breaking his longtime lover, who couldn't stop wanting to let him go? What does it take to decide to leave—and survive?

Betsy's learned one of the leaving lessons early, Bruce recalls. He sees her review it as she struts her hipbones to stage left, and Mr. Albee jabs a note into the script that he carries on his lap, which will involve a scolding.

But now she's 8 years old and in Heidelberg with her father, with her American-born mother, having left the town of Arnsberg that she can never love enough, its chorusing forest of whine, creak, crack, their stone house so wide that a day goes by before you find it possible to sniff through every inch of it and that Betsy won't, ever again, choose to stand up in. They've come in 1939 to give a goodbye to what her father doesn't want to forget, before his people, their people, ravage more lands and borders and persons than anyone could own the strength to count. Her father hikes her along what he wants to call a mountain but which looks like a hill, where the broken castle lies, numbering the time that spirals away from it. The castle's stone, gold though seamed with grey, forecasts what will happen to her hair when she's between husbands, many years on, her two children grown and gone to an elsewhere, without her. Betsy's father is pointing at the Neckar that bends its arm around the city, at those pines high on the water's other side, their needles cricket-green under snow that swoops down in a kind of time-lapse, flake by flake, her way. Booted across an ocean and in a Manhattan whose language she can't yet master, Betsy doesn't want the Germany that her father offered her. She wants anything except this self, inside which her parents raised her, even Mrs. Prentice, so busy scrambling for love that she never thinks to ask what might be given back to it.

What Bruce doesn't want is the fire that yearns only for its own heat. He doesn't want the smile that Mr. Albee flickers at his rumored bedmate of the month, at the aptly named Randy, who gets his coffee and sharpens his pencils and whose actions appear to bargain on the words, Do for me, and I'll be done by you.

Bruce wants some mixture of Betsy's vertical and horizontal people, as if a person could be a chord that you stare at, standing up straight on the parallel lines it clings to, the movement of its voices changing the whole that you thought was there.

The Snowy Linden

They roll a water-damaged piano out into the courtyard. They've listened for a while, in passing, to the sound of paired bodies sticking together in the backstage shadows, most married to others partners. It's hours after the last of Mr. Albee's upbraidings, leveled at fumbles that will be righted tomorrow night. The moon wavers plump above the linden. Its leaves start to rustle, though no wind stirs to push them. Betsy's in a chair against its trunk, while Bruce plays on a cluster of chipped keys, testing their tunefulness. When she asks him to give her that song by the reedy woman who wishes she'd stayed a painter, he knows Betsy means how its ache can quiet Orton's words, chattering in her head. She heard Bruce hum a few bars in the morning, and the melody's rising curves fixed her in a doorway from which she couldn't move, for minutes that she remembers now. Joni Mitchell's "Willy" hymns about a man gazing through his lover's window, unsure of his capacity for yielding to the woman next to him, afraid of finding himself like the moon outside the glass, conquered by human footprints and staked, as if he were turf. It's about those few opening chords, moving up and down in a narrow space, gradually expanding over the piano's range and that voice leaping widely to show how high answered feeling will take you, if you follow.[9] Betsy concentrates on the slide of Bruce's voice, up, up, when she sees herself, years after the death of her second husband. She sits in their Upper East Side apartment as a nurse feeds her the soupy lunch that she can manage, in a once unlikely 2015, spring flaring at the windows. The music whose source she can't discover sings in the lone world that her eyes admit her to, at 83, and it's like sucking on a cut lime. You wake to the tart that lives in your mouth and submit to the greenness that makes a smudge of everything, later. At this moment, Bruce, who'll never again be the boy or Bran, arches up his throat, about to reach the height of Mitchell's vocal line on the words, *And I feel like I'm just being born / Like a shiny light breaking in a storm*, while a magpie varies its grumbly song, which springs onto a steep pitch and holds there. The linden's a shower of snowy petals on the piano lid, on Betsy's hair, a sugared muskiness pooling in the grass. Betsy and Bruce think of what it can mean to stand on the ground that carries every weight, the weights in the boom that the body fashions before the name of love, the weights that slam beyond hurting, those that nearly break the ones who consent to bear them. For hours, they know, the moon will speed down its stolen light, beaming over all of it.

---

[9] Mitchell's use of the piano, its rolling and warmth and sometime friction of its chordal tensions, along with the movement of those tensions, helped me to enlarge my sense of the possible: the piano sings as it accompanies the wide-leaping voice. And at the age of 11, when I first heard Mitchell play, all this was like standing in a room, the light ablaze and always on.

The Life in the Sky Comes Down Essays, Stories, Essay/Stories

Twenty

The Life in the Sky Comes Down Essays, Stories, Essay/Stories

Shake the Palsied Heart

On this late Sunday night, halfway through July, I listen to the wood thrush outside our kitchen window. His song's upward curl fills the back garden two stories below, butts against the humid air, and makes all of Brooklyn's Cobble Hill his sound. Behind me, in our bedroom, the man I've loved for 15 years sleeps with the AC droning on high, preparing for a dreamed apocalypse with moans and grunts that rise from the sheets like sonic spume. We've been watching *Fortitude*, a British-backed/Icelandic series involving a town on the edge of that glacier that's melting to a sped up tempo. A young girl and boy find a wooly mammoth's carcass, whose tusks shoot up from the almost slush. They touch the point of each spear, and everything goes aslant: all their neighbors, overtaken by a virus older than prehistory, ruin those they love the best, the lovers, the husbands, the wives, the children running red amid the ice-melt, as if this ancient, taken thing could only scourge the ones who thieved what ice should never have given back. I'm leaning into a beyond kilter world, misordered by a rhythm I don't yet know how to see, thinking of that man who wheeled his truck down the promenade in Nice and pulped 84 bodies for nothing I can recognize, while fireworks still flurried in the sky that went on, above. I'm thinking of American guns that hypnotize their owners, of bullet sprays flashing in an Orlando club, through the policed streets, for nothing I'm willing to consent to, of brown bodies that can't stand up from what put them down. I'm on the verge of 60, if 60 has a verge, an age I never thought to live to, stalked, like so many, by a virus whose push through the 1980s made every stretch of land a gravestone for the lives of Luiz, Douglas, Stuart, Patrick, Walter, Chris, men I seem to see at moments before our bedroom windows, as if my longing could hold them up. I close in on the palsy that can ride over the heart, if you let it, if you don't know how saying no to it must be possible, that pumping stopped, stilled, just before making contact with the outside you live in. In a worry at what it means to deny the palsied heart, stoppered by too much feeling and not enough feeling and a terror of feeling's keenness blunted over time, I meet the image of George Whitman.

I'd come to Paris in 1983 with a stash of bills saved from jobs I hated, selling overpriced art supplies in Boston, overpriced clothes in Greenwich Village, trading on the shaping wonders of Bach and Satie with students who yearned to get each note into every finger, so that music might beat in a haven there, an exchange I hated less because what we traded cost so much more than my fees for teaching it. George, in my first view of him, stood astride the front door of Shakespeare and Company as if he were a gate, locking out any person likely to stir a grumble, growled at someone who, George knew, couldn't care enough for the practice of bringing the mind to settle in words on the printed page.[10] I saw his brown corduroy jacket 3 times weekly for 4 years. Elbow-patched, salt/shiny, it was as under-cleaned as the store behind him, a ziggurat of books lacking a temple at the top, unless George's apartment just under the sky served that purpose. He'd owned the place for more than 30 years. He'd cleared 70, hired me to work at inventory, to run the cash-desk, to hand-pick with his approval who would read poetry or prose on Monday nights. His gaze on the street hung over its 12th century origins, the logs trundled in from Normandy and unbound by the brownish river, a little later, the butcher-meats spoiled beyond selling, tossed to men and women somehow their equal, what would never be bought tugged by hands that could do anything but pay. I thought, often, that this history of spoilage, this diminishment of trees and flesh, hexed the place that George called his own. Yet Sylvia appeared and reminded me that it's the business of stories to change.

All of us in the bookshop had the tale of Sylvia and her genesis, or we mistook that sequence for the girl who must have sprung from it. Felicity, her mother, began in the Highlands, in a craggy castle whose

---

[10] Over the years, I came to understand that the *no* George seemed to stand for, the *no* committed to gauging the level of care and precision at work in those he met, made even deeper and more ample the *yes* multiply ringing on the other side of it.

windows rattled their melodies in wind that never stopped. And stopping became a theme: her father, the marquess, berated Felicity for that camera around her neck, for how she'd vanish among the grasses while photographing the crofters with their sheep, in their dim rooms, by the lake that ate the sun when it was low and fat and sinking. Refusing to be stopped, to plant herself at the appointed time, in the right room, before the right man whom her father was hustling her to marry, she arrived in Paris and discovered something else. She saw a George in need of tidying. She saw the nearly 50 years between them and that he wouldn't force her to stay his junior. She could clean the floors of books and brutalize the bedbugs in the upstairs reading room with aerosol and craft a kitchen for George in his apartment, where a hotplate stood, by a window so smeared with time that nothing glinted through it. But Felicity confused the man who quivered at the sight of her with the George who never happily quivered for very long. There was always another door to yank from its hinges, so that his top floor would be one widening place, a series of thresholds giving out to signed first editions available to every hungry hand at every weekly party. After marrying George, after birthing Sylvia, Felicity left her to the dirt. Yes, 6 years later, she pulled her daughter from the chaos that trumped her plans to order it. Yes, at 22 and London-schooled, Sylvia returned to a father, now 90, who conceded that she should remake what Felicity had failed to. But during my time among the books, Sylvia carried bits of the world in her hair, plane tree twigs, mud scooped from the Seine on the Quai's other side, a smile at her mouth like a light, rimmed by the chocolate there. At a moment in this family drama, George noticed my dread of what it covered over. He liked my horror, he said, but get below it. Get under it. That's where the unsticking starts.

    The quest to unstick joined me at one of our storemates' parties in the Marais, where the marsh was gone too long, though its ghost wobbled air into waves. Mathius, Adik, Dominique, Simon, and I: we left 4 continents behind us for the honor of moving through the gateway into George's domain, proceeding as if the past could be bundled, abandoned, as if the past didn't have legs. We were going to henna each other's hair in a townhouse owned by a count on vacation with the wife and 2 daughters he couldn't talk himself into wanting. The count belonged to Simon's dalliances, as he called them, coupled with for the moments it took to swap a sufficient pile of francs to cover the rent that lay beyond Simon's ability to manage it. With eggs and lemon and henna on our heads, a martini in every right hand, I noticed Sonya. She was closer to the ground than she liked, had Louise Brooks bangs and pink shoes with silver buckles on her feet. Simon admired Sonya for what she trailed with her. She had an army of tiny metal men in her bag, dressed in Austrian uniforms from the 1840s. We stood in one of the count's corridors that bent like a forearm, the bubble glass windows forming a pattern of raindrops paused on each rectangular ledge. As she told me that Belgrade was the home she'd run from, that her country would blow higher than any cloud in the 1990s because of the lives that balked at neighboring one another, she began her display. Sonya arranged her men in war-ready stances, cannons poised, guns lifted, death encircling all the buttoned torsos. She played at the future desolation that was her terror, with old toys whose prophecy would be proved. Later, the lights clicked off, we frisked at hide and seek throughout the count's rooms, and Sonya discovered a closet stuffed with sex dolls, inflated boys led by trunk-long cocks, each eye painted a faded blue, staring, as if alarmed by prickly lashes. We were in what Simon clung to as our mid-ish twenties, the dark around us, afraid of being found. Flying back a week later to that America whose noise I didn't know how to hear, the listening was what I'd try for.

The last bookstore reading that George and I agreed on was Lawrence Durrell's night, set for a Sunday due to the rigor of his travel plans and because he was 75, belly-stooped, yet game for some of George's stew. That concoction pooled together the week's leavings, browned turnips, carrots gone elastic and so shaved, a few wrinkled peas, the leather-colored liquid they were doomed to live in frothing over the hotplate in a battle to get out. Durrell read to a crowd spreading across the first 2 floors, clustering on the stairs. He hit each word hard, new ones about Gnostic plots and conspiracies so delectable that you could taste them, their pieces, as they fit, outlining solutions delayed, always further on. It was important, he told me upstairs, after surviving the stew and when the dark stretched closer to morning, that his listeners not think of him as a mausoleum, the tomb out of which Justine and *The Alexandria Quartet* walked, that woman who wildfired his name through the forest of the world but who wouldn't die, who fed him when the books that followed her undersold and who, akin to the Kabbalah, adhered to the tradition to be read again, to be read under, like the surface she toiled at burnishing. We guided him to his cab, George and I, braced by our arms for the steep tread down. And by the fountain outside the shop's front windows, George raised a finger at swallows wedging wings into air, imprinting their shapes in it before whirring on, as if another world abided inside this one, was enfolded inside this one, whose briefness could be sighted if you squeezed up your eyes. I left him that evening for the country whose need to be read under I'd work at loving, Justine somehow in the seat beside me, like a thought.

    Years after George's slide at 98 into that near but other world, I'm on my way to our bedroom. My long-loved man is about to shout at the vision of primordial ice, at its slosh into an ocean that can't decline the gift. Waking him after a few minutes, I'll say that we must make ourselves the caretakers of nightmares, all of us who suffer and sometimes stand up from them. We should watch over the monsters assembled by our fear, assume the fortitude to guard against their power to savage this green ground whose harborage lies beyond dreaming. I know that the labor of watching over our internal and external ghouls won't stave off trucks careening down promenades to flatten the human life there, won't urge spent bullets to go back, to retreat into the gun that was their host, won't collect the slop of glacial waters and restore them to their once frozen source. Any upright vigil can be attended by the mess that takes time to read. But, like those messes that flourished in George's wake, we'll have to share them. I'll thump out the shaking of my heart when the wood thrush flexes his voice up through the trees. I'll see sunlight as a translucent bowl overturned on the garden, primed for the offspring of the day.

The Life in the Sky Comes Down Essays, Stories, Essay/Stories

Acknowledgements

The essays, stories, and essay/stories in this book have appeared, in altered form, in the following publications: *Out Magazine*; *Open Democracy*; *3:AM Magazine;* the *Journal of Speculative Philosophy*; *Cleaver Magazine; The Battered Suitcase*; *The Tusk Magazine; The Nervous Breakdown*; *Environmental Philosophy*; *Gargoyle Magazine*; *Word Riot*; *Pif Magazine; Able Muse Review*; *Glasschord Magazine; State of Nature Magazine*; *The Write Room; BlazeVox Magazine; The Fringe Magazine*; and in *Fogged Clarity: An Arts Review*. I thank the editors of all these, especially Ben Evans and his *Fogged Clarity*, because both connect thinking and feeling at the service of what can be made of them.

    I give a resounding thanks to Gretchen Heffernan, of Backlash Press, for what she and the press do in a world that needs more critical thinking and feeling, combined, than it will ever know. And I salute, heartily, Gretchen's wondrous imagination.

    I couldn't have committed myself to this book without the support of my colleagues at New York University, where I have been teaching writing, now, for 20 years. I thank NYU's Expository Writing Program's directors, Dara Rossman Regaignon, Denice Martone, Ben Stewart, Bill Morgan, Stephen Donatelli, and especially my faculty-mentor colleagues: Nicole Callihan, Amy Hosig, Beth Machlan, Mike Tyrell, and Ethan Youngerman. Thinking with you has been one of the great joys. Among the students with whom I've been privileged to think, write, and labor on behalf of crafting essays, I thank, deeply: Sam Barder; Hailey Bobella; Heather Dupire-Nelson; Sam Holloway; Dania Hueckmann; William Iffland; Erin James; Siri Loken; Tori Metcalf; Arthur Nottenburg; and Anthony Parks.

    Years ago, during a tough time, my friend Tom Lecky urged me to keep up with the words. I honor that urging, the man who made it, and the friendship that all this stood for.

Many words in this book have been surrounded by the life and death of loved ones, however invisibly, at whatever distance from me, given that some of them died of what Prince calls, in "Sign 'O' the Times," a "big disease with a little name": Michael Bromley; Betsy von Furstenberg; Douglas Harnden; Kevin Jones; Harvey Kaplan; Lisa de Kooning; Christopher Kosmas; Walter Seim; Luiz Silva; Stuart Smith; Beatrice Straight; Chanh Sisattana. You enriched the lives of everyone who touched you.

I thank my mother, Patricia Hamlin Bromley, for still sharing, at almost 95, in the joy of words with me.

My weightiest gratitude goes to my sister, Leslie Bromley Kaplan, and to my partner of nearly 16 years, Neil Merrick: here's to the life-music that we go on making.

Works Consulted

Banathy, Bela H. *Designing Social Systems in a Changing World*. NY: Plenum Press, 1991.
---. *The Guided Evolution of Society*. NY: Plenum Press, 2000.
Beauvoir, Simone de. *Le deuxième sexe*. 2 vols. Paris: Gallimard, 1949.
---. "Moral Idealism and Political Realism." 1945. *Philosophical Writings*. Trans. Anne Deing Cordero. Ed. Margaret A. Simons. Chicago: U. of Illinois Press, 2004.
Bell, Quentin. "A Cézanne in the Hedge." *A Cézanne in the Hedge and Other Memories of Charleston and Bloomsbury*. Ed. Hugh Lee. Chicago: U. of Chicago P., 1992.
Berger, John. *And Our Faces, My Heart, Brief as Photos*. 1984. NY: Vintage International, 1991.
---. *Understanding a Photograph*. Ed. Geoff Dyer. NY: Aperture, 2013.
Bertalanaffy, Ludwig von. *General Systems Theory*. NY: G. Braziller, 1968.
Cézanne, Paul. *Pommes*. The Provost and Fellows of King's College. The Keynes Collection, Cambridge.
Engelmann, Paul. *Letters from Ludwig Wittgenstein, with a Memoir*. Trans. L. Furtmüller. Ed. B.F. Guiness. Oxford: Basil Blackwell, 1967.
Fortitude. Series 1. Created by Simon Donald. With Richard Dormer. Sky Atlantic, 2015.
Hardy, Thomas. *The Complete Poetical Works of Thomas Hardy*. Ed. Samuel Hynes. NY: Oxford UP, 1982-1985.
Hillman, James. *A Terrible Love of War*. NY: Penguin Press, 2004.
James, Clive. "Technique's Marginal Centrality." *Poetry Magazine*. January 2012.
Jonas, Hans. *The Phenomenon of Life: Towards a Philosophical Biology*. 1966. Chicago: Northwestern UP, 2001.
Kramer, Larry. "A Lion Still Roars, with Gratitude." *The New York Times*.

May 21, 2014.
Lacan, Jacques. *Les Complexes familiaux dans la formation de l'individu*. Paris: Navarin, 1984.
Lanham, Richard A. *A Handlist of Rhetorical Terms*. Berkeley: U. of Cal. Press, 1991.
Lee, Hermione. *Virginia Woolf*. NY: Knopf, 1997.
Levi, Primo. *The Periodic Table*. 1975. Trans. Raymond Rosenthal. NY: Schocken, 1984.
Merleau-Ponty, Maurice. *Phénoménologie de la perception*. Paris: Gallimard, 1945.
---. *Le visible et l'invisible*. Paris: Gallimard, 1964.
---. *The Visible and the Invisible*. Trans. Alphonse Lingis. Chicago: Northwestern UP, 1968.
Mitchell, Joni. "Willy." *Ladies of the Canyon*. Reprise. Warner Bros. Records. 1970.
Murdoch, Iris. *Existentialists and Mystics*. Ed. Peter Conradi. NY: Penguin, 1997.
---. *Metaphysics as a Guide to Morals*. NY: Penguin, 1992.
Nelson, Maggie. *The Argonauts*. Minneapolis: Graywolf, 2015.
Nietzsche, Friedrich. *On the Genealogy of Morality*. 1887. Trans. Carol Diethe. Ed. Keith Ansell-Pearson. Cambridge: Cambridge UP, 1994.
O'Brien, Edna. Epigraph from *The Mountain Wreath*. 1847. *The Little Red Chairs*. NY: Little, Brown, 2015.
Plato. *Cratylus, Parmenides, Greater Hippias, Lesser Hippias*. Loeb Classical Library. Ed. G.P. Goold. Trans. H.N. Fowler. London: Harvard UP, 1977.
---. *Ion. Early Socratic Dialogues*. Trans. Trevor J. Saunders. NY: Penguin, 1987.
---. *Philebus*. Trans. Robin Waterfield. NY: Penguin, 1982.
---. *Protagoras and Meno*. Trans. W.K.C. Guthrie. NY: Penguin, 1956.
---. *Republic*. Trans. Sir Desmond Lee. NY: Penguin, 1987.
Prince. *Sign 'O' the Times*. Warner Bros. Records. 1987.
Proust, Marcel. *Contre Sainte-Beuve, précédé de Pastiches et mélanges et suivi de Essais et articles*. Ed. Pierre Clarec avec Yves Sandre. Paris: Bibliothèque de la Pléiade, 1971.
Purcell, Henry. *Dido and Aeneas*. With Lorraine Hunt Lieberson. Cond. Nicholas McGegan. Libretto by Nahum Tate. Philharmonia Baroque

Orch. Harmonia Mundi. 1994.
Robinson, Marilynne. *Absence of Mind: The Dispelling of Inwardness from the Modern Myth of the Self.* New Haven: Yale UP, 2010.
---. *Home.* NY: Picador, 2008.
Ruefle, Mary. *Madness, Rack, and Honey: Collected Lectures.* Seattle: Wave Books, 2012.
Snider, Sarah Kirkland. *Penelope.* Lyrics by Ellen McLaughlin. Performed by Shara Worden and Signal. New Amsterdam Records. 2010.
Sophocles. *Antigone. Sophocles I.* Trans. David Grene. Chicago: U. Of Chicago Press, 1991.
Stryker, Susan. "My Notes to Victor Frankenstein." 1994. *The Transgender Studies Reader.* Ed. Susan Stryker and Stephen Whittle. London: Routledge, 2006.
Strout, Elizabeth. *Olive Kitteridge.* NY: Random House, 2008.
Talking Heads. "This Must Be the Place." *Speaking in Tongues.* Sire Records. 1983.
Weil, Simone. *Attente de Dieu.* 1942. Paris: La Colombe, 1957.
---. *Cahiers.* Paris: Plon, 1970.
---. *La connaissance surnaturelle.* Paris: Gallimard, 1950.
---. *La Pesanteur et la grâce.* 1942. Paris: Plon, 1947.
Wiman, Christian. *My Bright Abyss: Meditation of a Modern Believer.* NY: Farrar, Straus, and Giroux, 2013.
Wittgenstein, Ludwig. *The Blue and Brown Books.* NY: Harper & Row, 1960.
Woolf, Virginia. *The Diary of Virginia Woolf.* Vols. 1-3. Ed. Anne Olivier Bell. London: Penguin, 1977.
---. "Memories of a Working Women's Guild." *The Captain's Death Bed.* NY: Harcourt Brace Jovanovich, 1978.
---. *Orlando.* 1928. NY: Harcourt Brace, 1956.
---. *The Second Common Reader.* NY: HBJ, 1960.
---. "A Sketch of the Past." *Moments of Being.* Ed. Jeanne Schulkind. NY: Harcourt Brace, 1985.
---. "Walter Sickert." *Collected Essays.* Vol. 2. Ed. Leonard Woolf. NY: Harcourt, Brace & World, 1966.
---. *The Waves.* NY: HBJ, 1959.

The Life in the Sky Comes Down Essays, Stories, Essay/Stories

Illustrations

Robert Littleford studied at the Royal College of Art, he now lives in Brighton with his husband and their Parson Russell. His work has appeared in major international publications including the Wall Street Journal, Washington Times, National Geographic, Vogue, Sunday Times Travel, Conde Nast Traveller, The San Francisco Chronicle and Canada's Globe and Mail.

The Life in the Sky Comes Down Essays, Stories, Essay/Stories

Biography

Bruce Bromley is the author of Making Figures: Reimagining Body, Sound, and Image in a World That Is Not for Us. He is a 2013 Pushcart Prize nominee for fiction and teaches writing at New York University, where he won the Golden Dozen Award for teaching excellence. His poetry, fiction, and essays have appeared in Out Magazine, the Journal of Speculative Philosophy, Gargoyle Magazine, Open Democracy, 3:AM Magazine, and in Environmental Philosophy, among many others. He studied piano, voice, and composition at the Berklee College of Music, earned his undergraduate degree at Columbia University, and his Ph.D. at New York University. He has performed his music and poetry throughout Europe and the US. The Oxford Theatre Troupe offered his play Sound for Three Voices at the Edinburgh Theatre Festival, where he performed the original score on piano, and his paintings served as the set.

The Life in the Sky Comes Down Essays, Stories, Essay/Stories

www.ingramcontent.com/pod-product-compliance
Lightning Source LLC
Chambersburg PA
CBHW022228010526
44113CB00033B/650